OKAY OKAY

OKAY OKAY

BY FRED KREBSBACH

Thank you for reading Okay Okay

ISBN: 978-0-9896710-1-9

Published and printed in the United States of America by the Write Place. Cover and interior design by Michelle Stam, the Write Place. For more information, please contact:

the Write Place
709 Main Street, Suite 2
Pella, Iowa 50219
www.thewriteplace.biz

DEDICATED TO:

Olivia, Cal, Charlie, Hailey, and Claire

TABLE OF CONTENTS

PREFACE

This book is about my experiences in Vietnam. I've had the privilege of being in the company of many WWII combat veterans, and one of the things that I've heard them say most often is how they wish they would have been more open with family members about what they thought of war and how their experiences changed their lives. They wanted to say something, but just couldn't or wouldn't. That's what I would like to do with *Okay Okay*.

Many have suggested I write this book, and I have clearly decided to do it; I do not want any of my grandchildren or grandnieces and nephews to ever have to go to war needlessly. Pace yourself and think it through. To think and not to panic were a big part of my actual combat experiences. I hope this book is different from the countless other books written about Vietnam. I love my kids, my grandkids, and my great other kids more than anything else in this world and respect the decisions they make in life about our country and service to our country. But I want them to think first and read on.

INTRODUCTION

Anyone who's been in combat has had many different experiences, as I did, but I would like to take a different approach. Many of the following chapters have some abnormality associated with them and many have a spiritual or a religious bent. I certainly don't wear any sort of religion on my sleeve, but the name of this book and my excruciating focus on attempting to think and not to panic, with a spiritual note, led me to constantly think about death or dying and resulted in me doing some really stupid things!

These are the kinds of things you never, ever forget, yet wonder why they happened the way they did—or you find yourself wondering "what if?" There is no politics, there is nothing to prove, no hidden messages, nothing learned, nothing gained, and nothing won or lost. Bullets, bombs, booby traps, napalm, Agent Orange, rockets, grenades, and faulty equipment don't have brains. I hope some of the following chapters demonstrate the basic instinct of survival soldiers have for themselves and for the guys around them.

Full disclosure: I never prayed but once, maybe, in Vietnam. No one was KIA (killed in action) in my squad or platoon by direct enemy contact during my entire time in the field, but many were wounded. All KIA were from booby traps. I carried the M60 machine gun and always

had two ammo bearers. The whole string of them would
be wounded or killed by booby traps up to the time I gave
up the M60. I did things differently than most with my
gun crew and it worked out well for all of us. I hope that in
the following pages I can show how the dichotomy of war
caused events to turn out as they did.

I carried the M60 just short of seven months before I
ended up in the hospital. When I returned to the field, I
gave up the M60 and was a squad leader for Special Forces,
which played out well for me and my squad. About this
time my emotions started to play havoc with me. If you're
wondering why, stay tuned.

One last thing—I will try to bring into focus the role
of my family and how it played out in both good and bad
ways. Yes, there was some not-so-good. But thankfully, the
majority was positive for me, especially when I was in the
field and when I returned home. Many people unknowingly
were lifesavers. My older sister was an outlet for me when I
was in the field, and one of my younger brothers was when
I came home. Neighbors, relatives—the whole community,
really—were instrumental in helping me deal with trying to
be a human being again, starting only thirty-six hours after
leaving Vietnam.

Some things, totally out-of-this-world to most, caused
the most emotional reactions in me and seemed to come out
of nowhere. It's funny to think about them now, but they
were truly important. I spent many nights laying in the
mud looking at the stars, hoping not to get killed, dreaming
that I would be able to go home and eat "turtle" with my

cousins Shelly and Harvey at Aunt Leona's and Uncle Gilbert's. After I made it home, I remember I sat down at the table with them to have turtle and I completely lost it. The emotions suddenly burst to the surface and poured out of me.

1

FRESH MIDWEST MEAT

NOVEMBER 1968—I HAD JUST turned twenty-one on the tenth and was ready to graduate from vocational school. The whole month was dedicated to interviews with job recruiters. My classmates and I were all through with classes, lab, and demos and were looking forward with excitement to the possibilities of employment.

I wasn't the brightest bulb in my graduating class (play on words...I had a tech degree in electronics); however, I was able to comprehend the concepts of the huge and rapidly expanding world of transistors. The saying went, "we are never more than two months away from being obsolete," so I had to keep up, and I liked it. I was one of only a few students who went to class for four hours a day and worked for eight. I worked the second shift at Pepsi Cola and started out as a bottle sorter. It was the best job I ever had. I learned it's not always the job but the people you work with. I paid my way through school, every Monday morning, one week at a time. I paid my rent and had a car to drive. I started out with a piece of junk but kept trading up for a somewhat better piece of junk, and by the time

I was ready to graduate, I had a pretty decent set of wheels. Just missing one gear!

I had also worked my way up to a position as a forklift operator in the shipping and receiving department. I always had good reviews and was part of a skeletal staff of people selected to open a new warehouse. We were to continue with all the Pepsi products and take over operations for a newly purchased Pabst distributorship. I thought I had a good thing going for me. I was graduating with a tech degree and I already had a resume with excellent references. But...no one would talk to me! One day, the RCA job recruiter from Indiana leveled with about fifteen of us graduates. He told us no one was going to hire us—we were all subject to the draft and companies were no longer hiring young graduates who were going to be drafted. If they did, they would have to provide jobs for them when they returned from active service. Employers already had too many employees in this situation. How right he was! It wasn't long before I was notified of an upcoming status change for the draft.

All indications were that I could expect my draft notice in the mail the first week of January 1969. Sure enough, when I checked in the fall of 1968, I was told that January 5 was to be my notification date. One of the Selective Service board members told me to get on the very next bus going out for draftees, leaving for the induction center in Des Moines the first week of December. He told me that I would only be gone about four days. I would get my shots, a haircut, and be sent home on Christmas leave. I wouldn't start basic training until January anyway and I would have already served one month.

Sounded like a plan. All I could think of, though, was that I had just turned twenty-one years old and I hadn't had any time to enjoy it.

I was such an idiot, though! All the time I was working and in school, I never watched any news and was totally uninformed. I didn't know or hear a single thing about what was going on in the world or, for that matter, what was even going on around me. Get this—I didn't know about Woodstock. I had no phone, no television, and I didn't write to anybody. I had to work; it wasn't acceptable to have five minutes of free time when you could be working instead.

Needless to say, the world around me finally caught up. For me, avoiding the draft was not an option. News to me was that there was a draft for the marines. I was at the induction center, following the red, yellow, and green lines, when I learned about the military cadre's unique way of drafting young men for the marines. They would just bark out orders and if anyone stepped wrong, looked wrong, looked sideways, was too slow, too fast, coughed, or did anything out of line, this jerk—and he really was a peacock—walked up to him and said, "Hey you, 'marine,' come with me!" My only other experience with the marines was when I was in the field in Vietnam and my company was called in as reinforcements. It was not a good experience at all and left my platoon with a lasting impression. I'll touch on that in a later chapter.

There was a guy on the bus to the induction center from my hometown named Tony. The two of us tried to stay one step ahead of the bullshit. But Tony flunked his physical and was immediately pulled out of line and sent home. There were about fifty of us that day from the state of Iowa who passed our physical without getting tapped to be a marine.

I weighed 149 pounds, my temp was 98.2, my IQ was 127, I had all my senses, I could read and write and knew math. At that point in the process, we were told that if we were swinging a dick and somewhat warm, we were fresh Midwest meat heading for "AIT." It took a bit before I found out what that stood for. We were already being treated as less than human—just "meat on the hoof." It was advanced infantry training.

Before that, we had to get through basic training. Not much to say about that except I met at lot of guys like me. I gained twenty-seven pounds, got in good shape, and came out looking like a little bull. We were all pretty much a bunch of country boys, so it didn't take two weeks of training for us to fieldstrip a rifle and put it back together again. After five minutes of that, it was all downhill. Everything was a simulation. Simulate throwing a grenade, simulate crawling under barbwire, simulate crawling under live fire—that was a good one—and simulate navigation. It was in basic training where I learned to "hurry up and wait," "smoke 'em if you got 'em," and "if you don't have 'em fallout for police call." And I would hear over and over again, "on your feet, meat."

I got off the plane in Fort Polk, Louisiana, where I was to start basic training. I remember it was a decisive moment for me. Induction cadre suggested that I wear old clothes when reporting for duty. There I was, in ragged clothes, old shoes with holes, and a big bulky corduroy overcoat that hung down to my ankles. It was three o'clock in the morning. I was all alone leaning against a tree and I was supposed to wait until someone came by to pick me up. All I could think about was that my draft notice said my friends and neighbors wanted me to do this and they even signed it, "Your Friends and Neighbors and We Thank You for Your Service." So, where was everyone else? It was cold that January morning leaning against that tree. I had lots of time to think. I thought, maybe I could just disappear. I was certainly dressed for it! As it was, I made my first mistake. I waited...

As time went on, I started to get answers to some of my questions. In basic training, the people in my platoon were white Bible-Belt farm boys, poor white Southerners, blacks, Mexicans, boys from the coal, fields and...foreigners!? I'll explain. The deal was if any foreigner wanted to join and fight in the United States Army, they could. In return, they would have access to the education promised in the GI Bill. These guys knew where they were going, and as I went through training, I began to realize were I was heading as well.

My involvement in basic training was low key, so I thought. I had a couple of buddies who were from Iowa, so we looked out for each other. But then things changed, and I was noticed. One particular day, my buddy Giles and I were marching in the very back of our squad. We were marching in small squad-sized elements because of the possible spread of meningitis. Our platoon was spread out over a wide area, and Giles and I were the last of the last.

As we were marching along, we went past the post barber shop. There was a woman leaning against the door smoking a cigarette. I don't think she had any teeth and she looked mean and nasty. She had on a dress and was scratching herself in various places with one hand and smoking with the other. Drill sergeants were calling cadence, so we didn't think they would hear us if we whistled at her. Giles and I let out a couple of "hubba hubbas" and a few wolf whistles, and then everything and everyone stopped. We were caught!

When one person, or in this case a pair, get caught doing something perceived to be "out of line," the whole platoon is made to suffer (ha). Everyone had to do push-ups. The idea behind this was that if the platoon knew they'd be punished for the bad behavior of others, everyone would police each other. Didn't happen. Everyone took one look at her and the whole platoon started laughing as we were all doing push-ups. The drill sergeants were not happy and made us report to the company commanding officer (CO). Talk about stupidity. This guy was a green horn captain and he thought he was important. He would strut around with his helmet high on his head, pulled down over his eyes, and his aviation sunglasses. He wore the light blue infantry scarf under his pressed shirt with one good conduct ribbon on his inflated chest. Giles and I were supposed to stand in his office and whistle for two hours! We drove him nuts after twenty minutes.

Coming as a complete surprise, my entire platoon voted for me to attend leadership preparation school. So, off to leadership prep. Once there, they made me a make-believe NCO (non-commissioned officer) with stripes and everything that goes with the title. It was a pretty good deal. I had my own room, better food, and I was learning something. It was during this stint that I started learning how the military works, and I began to wonder if I should try to be smarter, act smarter, and even out-smart military leaders. Maybe it was intuition, but it was easy to anticipate their every move and intent.

At the end of leadership prep I was approached by the cadre commander. He wanted me to consider going to Airborne School and officer's training at Fort Benning, Georgia, and he would facilitate my transfer. I thought about it, but I turned him down. I didn't want to get any more involved with additional training, I didn't want to jump out of a plane, and I didn't think I wanted to be a "Screaming Eagle." I knew it was only a "shake and bake" school, anyway—it would probably be a thirty-day deployment, and you'd come out a commissioned or non-commissioned officer. The army would assign these guys to the battlefield rather than an invested officer. They were still just "meat." It was a faster track to a promotion, but you had to make it out alive from the jungle.

After graduating from leadership preparation school, I was assigned to be a squad leader for a new bunch of guys for—you guessed it—AIT. Damn. All of a sudden, jumping out of a plane didn't sound so bad.

AIT was much the same as basic. Instead of having classes for two weeks to learn how to fieldstrip and re-assemble a M14, now we had to do it all over again with an M16. That took all of five minutes! AIT was a joke. But it was a life-changing experience. The guys I trained with were the guys I would go to Vietnam with. Many would not make it back alive.

As a squad leader in AIT, I shared a room with the other squad leader of our platoon. His name was Rameshchandra J. MacWan. He was from India, and he was a pretty good dude. He had difficulties with his squad, though. There was already a lot of racial segregation and separation. These were early signs of what was to come. There were fifteen guys in my squad, of every color and class. I got along well with everyone, probably because I didn't fall into the military mold. A couple of my guys got very sick, and I did whatever I could to get them immediate help and into the hospital. The whole squad worked together to help, and that brought everyone closer together.

Of the fifteen guys in my squad, there were a half-dozen black dudes. One was a guy named Washington, and he didn't live too far from base. He was married and had two small kids. It was my duty every day to do a head count every time we were told to fall into formation, as well as bark out orders—FALL IN, FALL OUT, REPORT, SOUND OFF, etc... Frequently, Washington would just disappear on a Friday or Saturday and not be back until the following Wednesday. I would bark out every day, "All present and accounted for." Then another man disappeared! More and more stopped showing up, but no one knew the difference and no one ever caught on. It got to be comical. If someone just didn't feel like it or if the weather was crappy, he would hide under the barracks until we had roll call and then leave. He'd hide out in the back of the mess hall and spend the day throwing butcher knives into the back of a big wooden freezer door, or sleep all day.

The reason I remember Washington is that he figured out what I was doing and one day he asked why. I didn't have a good answer for him. I told him that one Saturday I knew he wasn't in formation and since it was a Saturday, for the hell of it, I didn't report it, just to see what would happen. Nothing ever did. I started to think the army staff didn't care, which reinforced the idea that we were all just meat. It was strange, because shortly after that, Washington was always present and accounted for. I sometimes thought he wanted me to report him as AWOL. Too bad he ended up in the "Group W" squad!

At this time, racial discrimination was still prevalent in the South. Remember, this was Louisiana in the 1960s. We all had leave coming after several weeks of simulated jungle training and took off for the nearest town of Leesville, aka Diseaseville. The first place we visited there was a bar. There were about eight or ten of us guys and McWan. The bar staff said he was black and wouldn't serve him. To make a long story short, we got kicked out of every bar or nightclub we went into. Eventually, we gave up, bought some booze, and went back to a party room at the hotel. We all got hammered. As the night wore on Mac decided he was going to call the embassy, the president, the Pentagon, and the Department of Defense... I can't remember if we ever managed to cool him down, or if he just passed out. The rest of us stayed up all night talking. Reality was starting to hit us in the face...the night turned quiet, but we were all wide awake.

We managed to struggle through the rest of AIT, even simulating throwing hand grenades. We were preparing ourselves. We knew our orders were being cut. There would be a short leave, and then we would report to Oakland, California, and from there to Tan Son Nhut, Republic of South Vietnam. The army had a unique way of preparing your family ahead of time. They would ask, very politely, if they would like to purchase an affordable life insurance policy for the young man going to Vietnam.

We knew we wouldn't have long to wait for our orders. Our drill sergeants were making plans to move on and couldn't wait for us to ship out. We had the feeling that if the army had its way, we would all be hung on meat hooks and shipped out on overnight freight to Vietnam. When our orders came, it was pretty anticlimactic. No one said good-bye. We shipped out on leave...many of us would meet again.

2

Leave

LEAVE WAS FOUR WEEKS LONG and everything seemed a bit surreal. I had lost track of a lot of hometown friends while I was in school, and quite a few had even already been to Vietnam. I tried to spend as much time as I could with a girlfriend, which I must admit was awkward. She was hinting at wanting to get married, and the more she pushed, the more I pulled away. I had an overseas tour of duty, and I wasn't sure about the outcome. I had an overpowering feeling that I needed to get through this next year and go from there.

I looked up some old friends and partied. I got picked up by the police in Cedar Rapids for "more things than I could ever imagine." A couple of hometown buddies and I had three girls with us that we picked up at a party after drinking half beer and half dandelion wine we bought at the Amana Colonies. I was driving my buddy's very hot muscle car, racing anything and everything and tearing up the town. All hell broke loose when I went flying through a downtown intersection—backwards. When I finally stopped and the smoke cleared, I looked up to see a cop stopped at the red light watching the whole thing. I looked at him and he looked at me and when he hit the switch to his lights, I hit the gas pedal. I must have had a dozen or so squad cars trying to catch me. I finally gave myself up in front of my buddy's apartment and they boxed me in. Once all the tire smoke cleared, they hog-tied me so enthusiastically that they had to carry me. My feet never touched the ground. They told me they were going to throw the book at me. But I had my orders with me, so they let me off. I realized afterwards how stupid I was. People could have gotten hurt. It was the first time in my life where I totally lost control of myself, and I think it had to do with where I was going.

My sister was in a convent, and she helped me through a lot. Maybe I felt she could throw some spiritual weight my way, for whatever it was worth. Certainly couldn't hurt! My little sister was at home, so I got to see her a lot. My leaving for Vietnam weighed heavily on her. She was great for me also. She had just turned eleven shortly before I came home on leave. She was always interested in what I was doing, or what was going on. There wasn't ever anything she didn't want to know. She always knew the exact minute when I would get home after a night out.

My two brothers were fifteen and eighteen. These two characters were more interested in cars and girls, but that was good too. They provided a little levity in my life. I put pressure on the older one to sign up for the draft as soon as possible. He had just graduated from high school and had no intention of going on to any further schooling. The army never sent two brothers to Vietnam at the same time, so it was beneficial for him to get in as soon as possible.

I visited with aunts and uncles, neighbors, and cousins, if I could catch up to them. I had several uncles who were WWII veterans and were able to prepare me for what I could expect going into a war zone. One uncle, "Red," told me to always keep a clear head and stay focused, to notice the little things, and to use my farm-boy ingenuity.

Another uncle, Gene, gave me the best advice. He said I should wear or carry something with me that would give me comfort in a time of need. I did just that and he proved to be right.

I had mixed emotions about my relationship with my parents. My old man, for all practical purposes, left when I was in the sixth grade. Then I failed seventh grade and struggled through all the other grades while doing most of the work on the farm. All we had was work—it was paramount over anything and everything. My brothers and sisters said, and still say to this day, it was almost a curse. I guess I was pretty bitter.

I never had much contact with my father, or, for that matter, any good feelings towards him. Sunday mornings he would appear at the breakfast table after we were done milking the cows, cleaning the barn, and doing other chores. We'd always end up in a big fight and he'd tell me to pack my bags and hit the road. We ran the farm without him until I graduated from high school and left for vocational school. My mother wanted me out and on my own. She sold the dairy herd a month after I left home.

When I was in basic training, the old man showed up to stay. He was home when I was on leave, and the only acknowledgement he made of the fact I was going to Vietnam was that he took out a life insurance policy on me. I felt I was worth more to him dead than alive. I wish I hadn't found out he did that, because I felt I would disappoint him if I came home alive.

When we were growing up, my mother cracked the whip. She was the straw boss and managed the farm. My brothers and sisters and I did the work. She was always concerned about all of us and did what she could, as she thought fit. The closer I got to shipping out, the more I could feel her falling apart. She was quite religious, and when things got tough she would say the rosary and light all the candles in church. I don't think that dang rosary ever got a chance to cool down. I never could understand what the big deal was about saying the dumb rosary. Saying the rosary never did a thing for me—nothing, nada, zilch.

As kids, we could knock a Hail Mary out in the blink of an eye. I even timed us once...three-and-a-half seconds. There are two parts to the Hail Mary. The first part starts, "Hail Mary full of grace...etc," and the second part, the response, starts, "Holy Mary mother of god...etc." When my mother started the first part, we immediately started with the response, and when she was done with her part, she would start right into the next. It was like a constant humming mumble. Sometimes, when my brother and I were younger, we would start cussing and swearing in a low mumble and no one would know the difference. We got the biggest kick out that, and even took the practice to church with us. We would blurt out the words "Holy Mary" then mumble, "pray for us no good #!?#X??#X! #!?!#??!!# dirty rotten sinners, amen!" I'll bet everyone in church thought those Krebsbach boys sure were a happy-go-lucky bunch!

I've gone on about this because afterward, my life and well-being took a major turn. After my uncle Gene told me to find something to carry with me in the field, I noticed my First Communion rosary hanging on the wooden spindle on the side of a mirror above my old bedroom dresser. I decided to wear that rosary around my neck with my dog tags and thought nobody would probably know the difference. That dang rosary took on a life all to itself from that point on!

The last night home, I went out with high school classmates, old girlfriends, upper classmen, and cousins, but I didn't want to make a long night of it. I wanted to be home early and to have the chance to get my mind set to go. Everyone was in bed when I got home. I could hear my mother crying and of course praying her rosary. The old man was home, but I didn't hear a peep out of him. Two buddies who were already back from Vietnam had offered to take me to the airport in the morning, which sounded like a good idea to me. They were coming about four o'clock in the morning to pick me up. It was a tough night though, no doubt about it. I was wide awake all night with a lot of thoughts and memories, and I had a couple moments where I completely lost it. My little sister's bedroom was just down the hall, and I could hear that she was awake all night too. When I left, I saw her peeping out of her door. I went downstairs and could still hear my mother praying and softly crying. What could I say? I quietly opened the bedroom door and whispered, "I'll see you later, don't worry." She was facing away from me when she reached back, and I just touched her fingertips with mine. I could feel her shaking a little, so I clasped her hand and left, closing the door on my way out.

I had said all my good-byes earlier to my younger brothers and to my little sister. My sister was crying. We had a big hug, but I didn't say anything. That was a tough one. What do you say to an eleven-year-old little sister, when it could be the last time you ever see each other? My two brothers didn't know what to say either. The three of us made the best of it. They just told me they'd see me later and to watch my butt.

3

VACATION CAPITAL OF THE WORLD/ SUNNY SOUTH VIETNAM

SHIPPING OUT WAS A BLUR. Many of the guys from my AIT unit were with me in Oakland, saying good-bye to family, friends, girlfriends, or wives. We had the usual hurry up and wait, following the line until boarding a plane. It was a commercial flight with the standard flight service and flight attendants. They were all easy on the eyes, but you could tell they went about their work with a heavy heart.

It would be a twenty-three-hour flight with a stopover in Japan. It was early morning when Vietnam came into view. From the high altitude, it looked like a beautiful country. It was so green with rivers and lakes, rice paddies, pineapple groves, and mountains with lush valleys.

The picture began to change as the plane descended. I was sitting on the left side of the plane, just ahead of the wing in a window seat. The plane started its big spiral descent, and the spiral slowly got smaller and smaller. Eventually, the Vietnam War we had all heard about hit us square in the face. We were prepared for a rough and fast landing. The flight attendants put on flak jackets and strapped themselves into their seats with full-harness safety restraints.

The more we descended, the more reality came into view. Helicopters were flying right below us and smoke was rising above tree lines from air and artillery strikes. This beautiful countryside turned into nothing more than thousands of bomb craters. As I was looking out my window, somewhat mesmerized by what I was seeing, I started to slowly and softly whisper a small prayer: "Angel of...God...my...guardian dear...to whom God's love...commits...thee...here...ever this day...at my side...to light...and guard...to rule...and guide."

I continued to quietly look out my window, when all of sudden, out of nowhere, deep down inside of me someplace, I heard as clear as could be, "Hooolyyy Shit!" I don't know where it came from—my logical brain, my emotional brain, or maybe even from my spiritual brain—right brain, left brain, or someplace in the middle. I must have been in a state of mild shock, because I clearly remember this, but I also remember not having much of a reaction either, except to say, "Yeah! To be continued..."

4

THE 9TH INFANTRY DIVISION

WE WERE TRULY IN A WAR ZONE, a fact we could easily see from the moment we landed. It was called "controlled chaos." As soon as our plane hit the tarmac, our anxiety level went through the roof. We were replacements, so we knew we would be immediately snatched up. I went into combat mode instantly...survival. We had already heard about the concerns and characteristics associated with each of the different infantry divisions, and none of what we heard was pleasant.

The word on the 9th Infantry Division was dire. From what I had heard, in no way did I want to be assigned to the 9th. The word was that if you didn't know how to swim, you shouldn't worry about being KIA—you'd probably drown within a week. The 9th Division was in the Mekong Delta and it patrolled the south, i.e. 4 core, relying on support from the navy, air force, and marines. Yes, marines! The 9th Division was the first in, not the damn marines.

The other concerns I had with the 9th Division were the rats and snakes. I hate rats and there were supposedly eighty plus types of snakes, all of which could kill you. Four of them did something even worse. Trust me, when you saw one, they put the fear of God in you. One of them, I don't know the name of it, was referred to as the "two-stepper." Then there was the "four-stepper," not to mention the stories of encounters with orangutans and tigers!

As we waited, a truck pulled up, and three of us were told to get into the back and be quick about it. The back window was out, so I stuck my head in the front and asked where we were going. "Dong Tam," he said. I asked what Dong Tam was. "Division headquarters," he shouted. "9th division headquarters for both infantry and mechanized."

Before I could process this, he handed me his M16 and said we'd be going through a couple of villages—nothing should happen, but just in case it did, I should shoot in the air and hang on for dear life. There should be some M16 ammo laying on the floor, here's a magazine. Put in what you can find, lock and load, and if anything is tossed in the back, jump. To me, this didn't seem like a great start.

We made it to division HQ without incident, but it was an eye-opener. Everything, and I mean everything, was scarred by war, with bomb craters in the road, pockmarks on the buildings, and everything covered with RPG fencing to protect what little was left standing. The sewage system was an open field or a rice paddy. The transportation system was a massive swarm of 50cc Honda motorcycles. That was the family vehicle, the work truck, the farm truck, the livestock hauler, the tractor, and as I would later find out, the transportation, shipping, and attack vehicle for the Viet Cong. One little 50cc Honda could take down a big deuce and half-military truck with no problem with any number of techniques, from throwing a grenade in the driver or passenger window, to launching a rocket-propelled grenade into the engine block or windshield, to blowing up the front tire or fuel tank.

We were off-loaded at a barracks for new replacements, which were temporary quarters because they were not forti-fied. We were told if there were a mortar attack, the sirens would sound and we should run to some massive bunkers for shelter and stay there until the all-clear was sounded. There were several barracks in a row, so I grabbed a bunk in the last one because it was the closest to a shower.

The showers were in a partly enclosed structure with a 500-gallon tank trailer called a water buffalo resting above it. Non-potable water could be pumped up to it, then gravity would feed water down to the shower heads, cold but wet. There were other replacement grunts already in the other barracks, and several of them would get stuck with kitchen patrol—KP—duty. This was a fancy name for a job that was mostly potato peeling and dish washing, but at least it was a good way to keep your mind occupied.

As soon as I got settled in a bunk, I went to take a shower, which actually felt pretty good. I came back to my bunk where there was your usual small talk, which lasted a couple hours into the night. All of a sudden, sirens started blaring. I imme-diately took off on a mad dash to the bunker, along with about fifty other people, all trying to get through a ninety-degree air-locked doorway at the same time.

It was totally dark inside, but I made my way to the back wall, where I sat down and didn't move. A lot of people were falling over each other and cussing, and some of it started getting racial and even more heated, until we heard the mortars start exploding close to us. We could feel the ground shaking. This was real.

I reached for my rosary and dog tags and they weren't there. It was then that I made my first really, really, really dumb move. I remembered I had hung them on a nail in the shower. I panicked. I thought if something happened to me, it would mean trouble because I wasn't wearing my dog tags, and more importantly, I needed that dang rosary. I got up and made it to the door, with people asking me what the hell I was doing. It was so totally dark inside that no one saw me when I slipped out. All I remember is that I ran as fast as I could for that shower, and I didn't hear any incoming mortars or run into any bomb craters.

The electrical generators weren't hit, so there was some light when I reached the shower. Sure as heck, there they were. Grabbing them in a flash, I took off for the bunker and made it back without anything happening. Again, it was so dark no one really noticed me when I slipped back in and sat down. It was then that I came to my senses and started to royally chew myself out for that stupid stunt. I was pretty shook up.

After a few hours or so, we got the all-clear. We returned to our bunks without a word. No one slept for the rest of the night. The next morning we got a firsthand look at the damage. The first of the three barracks was hit and had sustained major damage.

It was amazing and certainly shocking to see what bomb shrapnel does to steel lockers and mattresses, not to mention the side of a barracks. There were bomb craters all around, a sight that brought everything into sharp focus. One had landed right next to the mess hall. Remember the guys that got stuck with KP duty? Two of these guys were wounded, among several others. They were in-country less than twenty-four hours, and they were already badly wounded and shipping back to a stateside hospital.

5

5TH BATTALION, 60TH INFANTRY REGIMENT

AFTER OUR ONE EVENTFUL NIGHT at division headquarters, we were immediately shipped off to brigade headquarters in Tan An. We would be assigned to a battalion at Fire Base Roc Kein. There were about a dozen of us new replacements, and as soon as we landed at brigade HQ, NCOs ran us through a jungle training course.

The course sent us through a rice paddy, across a dozen or so paddy dikes, and across a couple of canals, all wired with trip wires tied to smoke grenades, which represented booby traps. We had to navigate mud up to our butts and were taught how to best help each other, what hand grip worked the best, and how not to get stuck. Needless to say, I tripped a smoke grenade right off the bat, which shook me up. Right then, I became convinced that a real booby trap was what was going to get me.

The smoke grenades weren't wired like you would think, with a wire stretched across a path. A lot of small string was woven into the mud so it would get wrapped around your boots until you eventually pulled the pin and it exploded.

Well, it gets worse. After a full day of this, they must have thought we were ready for the field. Each of us was assigned a tower for guard duty that night with five other guys. Thank God they knew what they were doing and that it was an uneventful night. We were still in the same clothes as the previous day, which was the norm.

At the end of the day, we were told to get ready to ship out to our battalion base where we would find out which company we were assigned too. We thought it would be a good time to take a quick shower. Just as we were about to jump in the shower, we noticed we were all covered in some sort of rash. I mean a big-time rash. These were some big blotches that looked nasty. The men who had been there awhile asked, "Didn't anyone tell you?" "Tell us what? What are you talking about?" Wearing underwear, socks, and a belt were a no-no. Any item of clothing that was a little tight would lead to "ringworm." We were covered in it. We were told that it's not actually a worm, but a parasite, and showering should take care of it in a few days. Just don't wear underwear and socks ever, and if possible, don't wear a belt when in the field. Then we should be fine.

It wasn't long before we were told where we were going. I and one other guy were being assigned to Alpha "A" Company at a base camp close to the village of Roc Kein. When we got there, it was nothing but one humungous, stinking mud hole. It was early June when I arrived, and guess when the monsoon season is supposed to start...June 1. I spent the next six months or more in the mud. I was attached to the second platoon of Alpha Company.

The platoon barracks was made of heavy wooden planks fortified with sandbags. The doorway was the usual ninety-degree angled airlock for shrapnel protection. When I stepped inside, it was almost totally dark except for one lightbulb dangling from the ceiling. There was about two inches of mud slop on the floor. The platoon was in the field except for a couple of guys. They said to just grab a bunk. Bunks were all the same, a steel frame with a rusted steel wire spring, and that was it.

Again, mattresses, blankets, and sheets were a no-no. I could see why! I made small talk with the two guys and found out they were short-timers waiting to go home. It was then that I found out five guys had just been killed. One was their point man and another, their medic. They had been well thought of. The three other guys were new. The medic, along with the three others, were killed trying to rescue their point man.

Four other guys would show up in the next couple of days from my old AIT squad. One was Hudson, and he would be attached to Alpha Company's second platoon. The three other guys were Moses, McNickel, and Mills, and they would be assigned to Delta "D" Company. Hudson was wounded after about three months in the field by a booby trap. It wasn't bad enough to be sent home, but he eventually ended up working in the motor pool. Both Moses and McNickel were wounded after about one month in the field. They both lost their eyesight. They were totally blind.

The fourth man, Mills, was a radio telephone operator—RTO—and carried the field radio for about eight months. One night Mills and his squad blew a major ambush and had to call in air support for help. One of our helicopter gunships accidentally fired on Mills and his squad. Several men who were standing right next to him took direct hits from rockets. He said he told them to take cover, and the next thing he knew, they were just gone, disappeared into a pink mist. They had set up their ambush site close to a small hooch. He was jumping around, the ground was exploding all around him, and big water containers were exploding everywhere, but Mills wasn't hit. He was never the same. He was a good RTO man, so he was able to get a job in the HQ communications room.

6

OKAY OKAY

THE 1ST AND 2ND BRIGADE were being deactivated and replaced with mechanized track units. The 5/60th was part of the 3rd Brigade, and many of the troops from the 1st and 2nd were being transferred to the 3rd. Many of these transferees were shipping in about the same time my platoon was coming in from the field, around the middle of my first day there. It was an eye-opener seeing these guys, who were some major-league hardcore combat grunts, bad-looking dudes, and realizing they were people I would be in the field with. They didn't acknowledge me at all except for a few disconcerting glances that sent chills up and down my back and made the hair stand up on the back of my neck.

As I mentioned before, it was already the monsoon season, so everything these guys wore or carried was a mass of mud. The platoon sergeant, Sergeant Bundage, or "Bundy," ran the show. He was a big black guy and your basic lifer, who had been busted in rank more times than you could imagine, but you knew right away you wanted this guy as your platoon sergeant. Everyone liked him and the more I got to know him

Nicky New Kid

in the next weeks and months, I did too. He announced to the whole platoon to get cleaned up, clean their weapons, and be ready to move out the next day. He then noticed the "Nicky-new-kid," aka Nick, and fortunately for me, he broke the ice. He had quite a time with me because of my shiny, just-issued green jungle fatigues!

My first night in the field is a night I will never forget. We were supposed to move out the next morning but plans had changed to late afternoon. I had learned something already. Plans changed constantly and you were told nothing of what the new plans were, or what we could expect. I was to be an ammo bearer and carry a box of M60 ammo on my back strapped to a big A-frame-type backpack. We moved out on trucks in a company-sized unit with all three leg platoons but without the mortar platoon. Mortar platoons didn't work out well during the monsoon season. I was handed a helmet and an M16, which was a piece of junk. All the weaponry had been handed down for years.

We unloaded along Highway 1, which the U.S. government had built from north to south. We moved down a narrow road that eventually turned into a narrow muddy dike where we met up with another company-sized force. We were to set up ambush sites flanking a wood line where there had been a firefight with VC the previous day.

I was in the second squad and we moved out across old rice paddies, crossing dikes and small canals. We arrived at a site that would provide two nighttime ambush locations for our squad. The plan was to move a few hundred feet further to our pre-nighttime location, sit tight until it got dark, then move back so as not to give away our position. Half our squad set up in a small brush line next to a duck pond. We set out claymore mines—anti-personnel explosive devices that could be detonated remotely if we had enemy movement. We had one radio, one starlight scope, one M60 machine gun, one M79 grenade launcher (thump gun), M16 rifles, and a 12-gauge shotgun.

We all stood guard until about 22 hundred hours, or ten o'clock civilian time. Then one person stood guard one hour at a time, monitoring the radio and keeping watch with the starlight scope. If there was any enemy movement at all, other ambush sites would be notified to get ready because our location was going to "blow a bush." We had been in our nighttime location for a few hours when sure as hell our RTO man whispered that he'd got the call that there was enemy movement in front of another location on our left flank.

I asked, "What we should watch for?" Our squad leader said to wait until they blew the ambush, then shoot towards the muzzle flashes. It was then that I again whispered to myself, "Angel of god my gua—" when I heard, "Okay okay, I know the words already!" I just laid there for a bit, when suddenly all hell broke loose. I didn't have a clue what was happening or what to expect. A few guys were shooting but our M60 man was not. I fired two shots in the air toward the muzzle flashes and quit. It didn't make sense to me because I didn't know if it was enemy fire or not. A voice popped into my head, saying I should sit tight, keep my head, and think it through. Just think, think, and think! I whispered, "Thanks!" This would happen again and again.

Rifle and automatic weapons fire was everywhere, and artillery started shooting flares into the air, lighting the whole area up. Several squads swept the area for any enemy KIA. Our squad leader didn't think our position was compromised but felt we should shift our position a little and move towards the duck pond, right next to the grassy area where we had originally set up our ambush site. We were lying right next to the water line, half in the water and half out, and we stayed that way for the rest of the night. It was horrible! We were lying in mud and duck shit. The smell was beyond belief. It wasn't until the next morning when we started to move out that a couple of guys noticed when I put on my backpack that there was a very dead, very ripe snake stuck on the back of my ammo box!

7

M60 Team

WE SPREAD OUT IN THE MORNING and patrolled a suspected infiltration area. When we returned to base it was early afternoon and nothing was planned for that night. There were quite a few new guys. I really can't remember why, but our platoon sergeant decided to reorganize the entire platoon. It must have been due to the influx of the other troops.

Later that afternoon Bundy stopped by and said he wanted me to carry the M60 machine gun. I thought this was strange due to the fact I had only been in the field one night and was a little small. We were told in AIT that the bigger guys were usually asked to carry the M60. But he wanted me to carry it with two other guys to help me out. They were named Shumate and Purvis, and they came over from the 2nd Brigade. They already had six months on line and were probably due for some time off; their feet were in bad shape. These two guys would prove to be invaluable during the next couple of months, and I credit them for keeping me alive. We would go through a lot together. Two other guys would be my ammo bearers, and the five of us would make up the second squad gun team.

Part of M60 and M79 Team – Myself, Reed, Weyant,
Fat Larry, and Smithy

We were told we would have a new second platoon leader, aka 2-6. This is radio code—2-6 was usually a West Point graduate with a commission, 2-4 was the second platoon sergeant, which was Bundy, 2-1 was second platoon, first squad, and 2-2 was second platoon, second squad. We would leave for the field again and when we returned our barracks/ bunker would have new lighting, the floor would have been scrubbed, all the bunks would have a mattress with new sheets, and we would even have a couple of fans for ventilation. This may have had something to do with the start of the monsoon season and our new 2-6.

I always had two ammo bearers with me at all times, and I really went through a lot of them. I lost all my ammo bearers while I carried the M60. One was killed by a booby trap and the rest were wounded by booby traps or enemy action. One of them would carry ammo for me for almost six months until he was wounded. His name was Weyant—he was quite a character and a good buddy. There were five of us in the squad that had been in-country about the same amount of time, so we were all good buddies.

We left for the field the next day and were out for some time. When we returned, we had been through several firefights and multiple ambushes that resulted in enemy KIA and wounded platoon members. The 9th Division it was known to make a lot of enemy contact, but it was with small elements of VC.

We made plenty of contact with the NVA (North Vietnamese Army), which had sizable enemy units. We were told during WWII American GIs were in combat with the Germans twenty-four days out of the year, which is what commanders said was the combat rate for the northern fighting zones in Vietnam. In the southern fighting zones we could expect to be in contact with the enemy "two hundred and forty" days out of the year. I learned there was a lot of pressure on the gun teams.

8

GI Ingenuity

THERE WAS THE EVER-PRESENT problem of faulty equipment. It was either defective or just plain worn out, but we kept using it.

Our new 2-6 was liked by some. He was from a long line of military brass and wanted to make a big name for himself. He volunteered our platoon to walk into an enemy ambush to engage them in small arms fire, while helicopters loaded with a company of troops were to land behind the enemy and call in artillery. It started out badly from the get go. First, we weren't told that our 2-6 had volunteered us for anything. We got hit and we returned fire. Nothing happened. No helicopters, no additional ground troops, and no aerial support or artillery. We knew nothing about this mission until the next day. We were all beside ourselves once we heard what our 2-6 had done. Later there would be more to this and a lesson learned for 2-6!

We had just started moving into what we assumed was our nighttime ambush location when we got hit. It seemed a little strange to everyone because it was highly unusual for this to happen just as it turned dark and strange to get hit with such firepower. We engaged with everything we had. My ammo bearers were just starting to belt together several belts of ammo when my M60 jammed! There was no quick fix to get it up and working. I felt I had not given away my position, so I just slid down behind a dike that was a little higher in one spot. It was probably less than two feet high, which is really a lot when everything is mud in the first place.

Purvis and Shumate slid down on each side of me to help. We popped the hood and everything inside went flying. There were gun parts everywhere. The primary buffer, buffer spring, receiver, yoke assembly, yoke clip—it was a mess. We were laying in several inches of dark, muddy water so we couldn't see or feel anything. Purvis pulled out his poncho and we all huddled under it trying to figure out what went wrong. We discovered a bullet had jammed in the chamber for some reason, which caused it to puke out all its internal parts. The bullet was sticking out maybe a quarter of an inch, but we didn't dare try to pound it in, as it would probably explode in our faces. Shumate had a cleaning rod so we tried to pound it out backwards and dislodge the bullet. All we managed to do was get the cleaning rod jammed. We couldn't get it to move in either direction, so we decided to find as many parts as we could that had fallen into the mud and put it back together as much as possible. We lit our cigarette lighters to search for parts. We found a few—the important ones anyway. We all peeked out from under the poncho and there were tracer rounds flying in every direction. We sat tight under that poncho and smoked cigarettes. I laid there for a bit and questioned myself "Okay?" and I heard another "Okay" right back.

We stayed in this position for some time until the shooting stopped. Then we were able to maneuver to a different location. It was clearly a hit-and-run by the VC. It was then that we got word through our RTO man that it was a botched operation. Artillery lit up the sky and word came for us to sweep toward a hooch area where the majority of the small arms and RPG fire was coming from. That was beyond unsettling. We did sweep the area and made it to another location to set up a defensive nighttime location. It's still unsettling to think about it even now. Shumate, Purvis, and my two ammo bearers moved in a horseshoe formation with me in the middle. They knew I was defenseless and could offer no support whatsoever. Luckily, we didn't come across any situation that would have required my support nor would we make additional contact with the enemy again.

The rest of the night we all stayed on alert, but it was uneventful. The next morning, reinforcements flew in to sweep the entire area for enemy movement, and eventually our platoon maneuvered back to our base. Once back at base, we learned that we had unknowingly walked into an enemy ambush with the intention of drawing fire. It wouldn't be the last time.

When we got settled in, my gun team went down to supply to turn in my M60. Once there, all of us, still stinging from the night before, made some changes. We explained our situation and started asking all kinds of questions. We learned supply sergeants aren't exactly quality-control specialists and don't care to be. We got a stern, blank stare when we asked if my

M60 had met any military performance specifications before it was cleared to be taken to the field.

If anyone has ever heard that the army uses the best and issues the best to its armed forces, don't believe it—it's a lie. The quality of weaponry is at least ninety-nine percent sub-par, and we found this was true throughout the entire battalion. We started our own quality-control effort, piecing together another M60. It was basic GI ingenuity that enabled us to do this. The credibility of the entire army supply business was suspect and corrupt. I'll explain later! We found all kinds of interesting things scrounging for parts. We disassembled a dozen or so other M60s until we felt we were able to assemble a fairly high-quality machine gun.

We found an asbestos bag shaped like a slender tear drop about two feet long including nice wide carrying straps. It was for carrying an extra gun barrel in the field. We found another gun barrel, and it ultimately became our own parts supply bag. This barrel bag became a vital entity unto itself for me and my entire squad.

We learned to do for ourselves, right or wrong. The supplies provided to us were always suspect if they were supplied at all. Our supply sergeant's name was "Frank Rank." No lie, for real. The word around about him was that he would be a millionaire once he was stateside.

A company-sized infantry unit was to consist of one hundred troops and was to be supplied every day with an SP pack. This supply pack contained everything one hundred GIs would possibly need for everyday activities: soap, shaving bars, razors, needle and thread, buttons, toothpaste, toilet paper, insect repellent, nail clippers, and of course cigarettes. Our company never was larger than maybe fifty guys in four platoons, with the fourth being a mortar platoon. The mortar platoon never went to the field and the three remaining leg platoons were made up of about forty guys at any given time. We might have seen two SP packs in a month. The word was that our supply sergeant would load a trailer about the size of a pickup box with SP packs hooked behind his jeep and drive to Saigon once a week to sell them on the black market. If this was true, we wondered what else he was selling on the black market that the enemy could get their hands on!

9

LISTEN TO ME

═══════════════

DURING MY ENTIRE TOUR OF DUTY, I can honestly say I was completely petrified twice. I don't know if I can say I was scared to death or out of control, but I was petrified—I froze. The first happened when we had been in the field for some time and had made enemy contact with both the VC and NVA on several occasions. We would "blow a bush" just about every night and sometimes twice a night. Sometimes we would blow a bush on the enemy and then they would hit us from the rear or our flank later on.

There were three companies on search-and-destroy operations in an area with a lot of enemy infiltration activity. There had been a huge battle between NVA forces in the area and one of our 9th Division track units, the 2/47th, just a few days earlier. We were moving through the battlefield and there were enemy KIA laying everywhere. We were on line, sweeping the area, which was a tangled, grassy swap, an open area with one small tree about three hundred feet to my right. As we were slowly moving forward, there was a huge explosion to my right about a hundred feet ahead of that small tree.

I stopped in place with my M60 at the ready, and then for the first time I heard the word "medic" called by the person who was hit. It was something that I'll never, ever forget...it was a scream, yet it wasn't; it was a loud shout yet it wasn't. It was panic, it was desperation, blood-cuddling, fear, lingering yet sharp, escalating but trailing off, dying but resolute. I still haven't found the right words to describe it. Our squad medic, Doc Howard, aka Doc Holiday, and two other squad medics took off running at full speed. That was what they did, defying danger.

It wasn't long before I heard what had happened. It was a booby trap. Like I said, we had been in the field for some time, but we had yet to come across a booby trap. It was my first, and I froze! I didn't know the guy, but as far as we all knew he made it. It took awhile for medics to tend to him and dispatch a dustoff, a Red Cross evacuation helicopter. It didn't make any difference; I was still unable to move except for getting down on one knee. I strained my eyes to the point that I think they actually hurt, looking for trip wires or strings.

Slowly the line started to move, except for me and my two ammo bearers. As the line to our right was approaching that small tree, there was an exchange of small arms fire. One NVA soldier was still alive and making his last stand. Some of our guys figured he was badly wounded but had been able to set a booby trap. Again, there was a pause and a chance for us to hold tight for a bit. I knew then that it was my last opportunity and to prepare myself to move. I was running out of options and there were still NVA in the area and they still had a lot of fight left in them yet. It was about then that my physical, emotional, and spiritual brain came together, and it took all three for me to take that first step. We had to move, period, so we started maneuvering! The next thing I heard was "Listen to me," which I assume was from the spiritual side of my brain. It didn't sink in until I heard again, only a little more forceful this time, "Listen to me—slow down, slow down." Well, my response was, "Okay okay!"

This first encounter with a booby trap broke the dam for many, many more to come. Booby traps would wipe out our platoon twice over and then some. In the short seven months I carried the M60, I know I lost a dozen or more ammo bearers just to booby traps.

10

Booby Traps

IT WOULD BE INTERESTING to know just how many booby traps we walked by, over, and under. We had a tiger scout named Rup assigned to our platoon. Tiger scouts were ex-VC that were captured and "rehabilitated," then assigned to infantry grunt units to walk point and to recognize booby traps like toe poppers, daisy chains, punji pit, and explosives. Rup was pretty good, and spotted most of them. We would move by them as quietly as possible before blowing them up from a safe distance. Sometimes we left them so as not to give away our position, and then when we were far enough away our forward observer would call in artillery.

Carrying the M60, I learned there were pluses and minuses to "humpin' the 60," or "humpin' the thump." One plus was that all the firepower, including myself, walked in the middle of the squad. One of my ammo bearers would walk maybe a couple of guys ahead of me and Weyant would always walk behind me, and then there would be the M79 thump gunner followed by our squad leader and his RTO man. Were we safer...maybe a little.

I thought one time I was a goner for sure. We were spread out, moving through an open area towards a wood line with a clearing about fifty meters ahead of us. Weyant and I were staggered about five meters apart, navigating water and mud up to our knees, when suddenly there was an explosion between him and me. I was thrown in the air. The last thing I remember seeing was my M60 suspended several feet above my head, then everything went black! I carried the M60 on my right shoulder when not at the ready and that booby trap exploded on my right side. My helmet flew a good fifty to sixty feet. I can't remember if I came to right away or while I was underwater. They plucked us both out of the mud and said we looked like the creatures from the swamp with two little white spots for eyes. My mouth was full of mud, my nose was plugged, and my right ear was packed with mud. It took us a bit to get our bearings back, and when we finally did, they found a bomb crater for us to wash some of the mud off. It was then we discovered we had lucked out. We didn't have a scratch—no blood, cuts, or holes. We all concluded that the trap had probably been set during the dry season, and because it was now monsoon season, it was covered with mud and water, which caused most of the blast to go straight up in the air, sparing us the full force of the explosion.

Only minutes later, as we continued on, part of the first squad and the front part of our squad sprung a booby trap that took out seven guys. It was big enough that it rattled everyone's clock. Two medics immediately went to work figuring out who was wounded the worst. Weyant ran to see who was hit, and when he came back he said that Tripp, my other ammo bearer, had been. He said our medic told Tripp that he was hardly hit and that he would be alright. He just had to sit tight until the dustoff Red Cross helicopter got there. After reporting, Weyant quickly went back to see what he could do, and Beck and I tried to help one of guys that was hit badly and struggling. We tried to do what we could until a medic could get to him. About this time, there were five of us who were good buddies—Addington, Anderson, Beck, Weyant and me. Even though we were replacements, we all had about the same amount of time on line.

Tripp took little of the blast to his front and had only a few wounds, but the guy who got it the worst was named Sprague. He had the proverbial "sucking chest wound." When Beck saw that wound he went, for lack of a better word, robotic. I look back on it now and I think it was Beck's way of coping. He sounded like he was reading from a medical journal. "What we haavvee heerree is an official suckingggg chest wound. We shall grasp the largerrrr of our aaaasort...ment of bandagesssss and with our thumb and forrrrefingerrrr separate the...plastic, beingggg carefulllll not to touch the side with which we are about to apply to the bub...bul...ling suckingggg chest wound while my aaaassistanttt puts pressure on theeee suckinggg chest wwwooound of the patient," until I said, "God damn it Beck, shut the hell up!" I didn't know exactly what to say to Sprague, but Beck was driving me nuts. I couldn't imagine what Sprague thought of it. Anyway, Beck and I started arguing and hacking on each other until Sprague began to smile at us and rolled his eyes. I found out he was from Des Moines, Iowa, so I immediately started to tell him about all the girls I knew there and that he should go look them all up.

Anderson, Weyant, and Beck

To our surprise, we managed to patch him up and to stop his sucking chest wound from bubbling. We covered everything, and I mean everything—there wasn't one hole we didn't try to seal off and cover. He was doing great and was able to walk with some help and was thanking us over and over again as we loaded him on the dustoff chopper. We loaded all seven guys on one chopper, including Tripp, and we thought he was the least wounded of all of them. We could see he was hurting too much to talk, but he was able to give us a small wave when the chopper lifted off.

The rest of our platoon managed to load up all the extra weapons, ammo, backpacks, helmets, and clothing, making sure not to leave anything behind for the enemy. We moved out of the AO to regroup without further incident. It was quite a hit for us to lose seven guys all at once, but it would happen again. Our platoon was down to ten, maybe eleven guys, so we really didn't want to get into a major firefight with any NVA or VC. We moved out of the area as quietly as we could and set up a defensive position while several other guys did a quick recon for possible nighttime ambush and pre-nighttime locations.

Once set up for the night, we took turns on watch, but no one slept. Everyone was quiet, but awake. It was the next morning that we got word everyone wounded the previous day made it except Tripp. They said he had died from "shock" during the night. They said he took one piece of shrapnel in the neck and that's what did it. That set us back a little, because we didn't think he was hit all that bad. Well, we just picked up and moved on and that's the way it was. Nobody said hello and nobody said goodbye. People just disappeared. More replacements were coming. I would get another new ammo bearer and again, nobody would say hello and nobody would say good-bye.

11

Eagle Flights

EAGLE FLIGHTS ARE HELICOPTER aerial insertion search-and-destroy operations. Our platoon went on eagle flights two to three times a week on planned search-and-destroy operations and two to three times a week if we were needed for reinforcement. It could be an adventure, because we were never told what to expect.

When choppers were coming into a LZ—landing zone—they didn't want to spend any time waiting for us to unload. A small observation two-seat helicopter called a loach would drop green smoke grenades if they thought the landing was friendly and a red smoke grenade if it was a hot LZ, which meant there was enemy activity in the area and to expect enemy fire. If it was an especially hot LZ, the chopper pilots would come in quite fast and initiate a fast-moving hover. We would all be lined up like ducks standing on both skids and just as soon as we thought it was slow and low enough, we would bail off.

I thought if I were going to drown, it would probably be from jumping out of a helicopter. During the monsoon season, many times we couldn't see the bomb craters because everything was under water. If we happened to jump off into the middle of an unseen bomb crater, all seven or eight of us guys would disappear underwater and our helmets would go floating across the water. It happened to me on a few occasions, but I was always lucky enough to be able to bounce off the bottom and not lose my M60 in the process. Most of the time the craters weren't that deep, but it was little nerve-racking waiting to hit bottom.

Some eagle flights were more raids than search-and-destroy operations. In a search-and-destroy operation you're looking for trouble, where as in a raid you're dropped into the middle of trouble. Raids are pretty hairy, because you're always set down in a hot LZ and sometimes you're fired upon before you get a chance to bail out. Many times when choppers were high and fast we would take our chances and jump rather than be sitting ducks. Then it was a good thing to land in the mud and water.

One operation in particular had a very hot LZ, and there were enemy VC in shining black pajamas running everywhere. We bailed out early when the choppers were fast and high, and when we hit the mud we were instantly stuck and getting hit with a heavy dose of small arms fire. No one could move, though no one was hurt when we landed. We had sparse but adequate cover to conceal us as we started to maneuver out of the mud. There was about ten inches of water that was quite clear, with a solid brown-colored bottom that we thought was sediment. We soon discovered it was solid leeches, which motivated us all the more to squirm and worm our way out

Eagle flights – Heading out

of the mud. I got myself unstuck with my usual method—the three-legged crawl, using one arm to pull while lifting one leg until I finally made it to a small dike were I was able to pull myself up.

Just then, as I turned my head ever so slightly, a green enemy tracer round went by within inches of my left eye. It was so close I felt the heat off it! I immediately dropped down behind that dike and laid still. That one was a close call. There could have been closer calls—I just didn't know about them.

Helicopter Cobra gunships came in and opened up with their mini-guns. They can shoot thousands of rounds a minute and use the same ammo I used in my M60 where every fifth round is a red tracer round. When Cobra gunships open up it's like watching red hail stones plummet from the sky.

Two other platoons were up close to the action and we were in the middle. It was the one and only time we came across an enemy hospital. As we got closer and closer it seemed like we were watching black ants running in circles. We came up on a navigation canal about seventy-five to eighty feet wide, lined with brush, elephant grass, and nipa palm with a well-traveled path—almost a small road—beside it. The platoon to our left was throwing concussion grenades in the water, and the current was fast and moving in our direction.

My squad and I were able to move right up to its bank and through the foliage for a fairly good view of the canal. It was at this very moment that black pajamas were popping up out of the water. The VC that were running around had jumped in that canal, and the current caused them to surface right in front of our squad. Two of them popped up right smack in front of me. As soon as they saw me, they started shouting "*Chieu Hoi*"—I surrender. I was shouting the same thing, and as we were shouting at each other, one of them brought his arms out of the water and the other didn't.

My squad leader yelled, "shoot, shoot." I almost opened up on them with my M60. There were other VC scrambling out of the water onto the opposite bank. The one who had not raised his hands disappeared underwater when I began shooting. We pulled the other one out of the canal, only to discover he was a she. About then, the Cobra helicopters opened up on the other side of the canal and the platoon to our right began tossing in more concussion grenades. My squad leader told me I had taken too big a chance by not opening up on them with my M60 sooner. He had been shouting for me to shoot, because he was convinced that the only reason the other VC would not raise his hands was that he was holding his AK-47 on me but it wouldn't shoot underwater, and I was staring him down with my M60.

The one we pulled out was a nurse; quite young, I thought, defiant, coal-black hair, shining black pajamas, barefoot, kind of small but in really good shape. There were many enemy KIA from that firefight, and more from the Cobra gunships and the concussion grenades. Of course the top brass had to have their damn body count! I thought maybe the action was slowing down a little, giving us a chance to regroup—and remove leeches—when things got even worse.

We had the one nurse POW and a number of other VC. There would be many more as well, as more units took POWs further downstream. Top brass were flying in with more choppers than you could image. They sure liked to come around when all the fighting was done and pull their "I'm in charge" bullshit.

It wasn't long after they arrived that their interpreters and several other tiger scouts they had with them started beating the living daylights out of this little nurse. It was pretty brutal. I can still see her getting beat up and rolling head over heels in the dirt. It got bloody. If this was interrogation, I didn't like it at all. She looked dead when they threw her in a helicopter. Throughout my time in Vietnam, this was the worst thing I'd seen. I looked away, and I remember saying to myself "Okay?" That spiritual spot in my brain, or guardian person inside me, hesitantly replied, "Okay?"

Eagle flights are very effective, but accidents happen in combat, like when thirteen people were killed when two helicopters collided on a search-and-destroy operation. The people included include our battalion commander, one general, chopper pilots, door gunners, and troops on the ground. We were already on the ground when we heard the crash. It looked like they were suspended in midair upon impact, before dropping to the ground in slow motion. The crash involved our battalion commander's chopper and a Cobra gunship, not a troop carrier full of other grunts.

Those of us carrying M60 machine guns and M79 grenade launchers were immediately told to secure the area while others in our platoon picked up body parts. I would eventually set up my M60 a good distance from the crash site when more helicopters with more troops were being deployed. Two guys from the third platoon had been killed on the ground. We were extracted when Special Operations took over. People who had been in the rice paddy picking up body parts had badly burnt legs from all the helicopter fuel floating on the water.

It was a terrible crash, but knowing the tactics of our battalion commander, many of us faulted him for getting himself and twelve others killed. We said he was "the uneducated wanting the unwilling to do the unnecessary."

It was unsettling and hard to accept for all of us. From then on, we tried to take control and manage our own combat operations on the ground, as well as our commanders flying around in the air over our heads. It turned into a game. We would pull some pretty crazy stunts on the ground and drive our commanders in the air crazy!

12

GI JOE

THE GI JOE COMIC STRIP, depicting a couple of WWII grunts in a combat situation living in a foxhole, hit home with us in Vietnam. It also dealt with their other buddies and their lives, like what their girlfriends—aka "Jodie"—were doing back home and family events, especially holiday festivities. It seemed like war and combat were repeating themselves, ironic, poignant, and reminiscent of WWII.

The worst thing about being away from home for me was hearing about someone dying. There was a delay between the time it happened and when I would get word that a family friend, a neighbor, someone's wife or husband, had died—or even worse, when I heard of the death of a young person killed in a car or farm accident.

I would just as soon have not known about any of it, but it was news from home, so I didn't have a choice. My mother—you gotta love her—would write to me about who died and which old "Jodie" was getting married.

I never asked her why she did this—maybe it was her way of having something to say. She would go on and on about who died, how they died, and how they looked: "Oh my, she looked so nice in her coffin. They did such a nice job on her, she had on a nice dress, you could hardly tell she was sick, and she was so young." Or, "He looked so good, so handsome in his coffin. Oh my, and he still had a full head of hair, he had on a nice suit, they did such a nice job on him you couldn't tell that there was anything wrong with him or that he had been ran over by a tractor and wagon, and he wasn't that old, either!"

There were "Oh so many people in church and the flowers were just beautiful, the choir sang the best ever, and his wife or her husband or the family was taking it so hard. And the food, oh my, we had so much food and was it ever good! Rosina Durban made her best ever salad and the desserts, oh my, all the neighbor ladies must have brought one." There I was, GI Joe sitting in his foxhole reading a letter from his mother about death and dying, scratching his head wondering why I was hearing this.

The best ones would be when she would write to tell me about old girlfriends...that Jodie was getting married and who she was marrying and how beautiful she would look with their picture in the paper announcing her engagement. Then the coup de grace: "She never would have wanted to marry you anyway," or better yet, "You wouldn't have wanted to marry her." That was my mother!

Once an old girlfriend of mine was getting married at the same time the girlfriend of one my buddies, Anderson, was getting married. The time difference meant that when they were walking down the aisle, Anderson and I would be in a nighttime ambush location. Anderson and I—GI Joe and his buddy—decided

Bringing in – Dustoff Chopper

we would take the hour watch together that was about the same time our old Jodies would be getting married back home.

We were near a suspected supply route of the VC. Our ambush site was fairly clear of any brush and wood lines, but we had tall elephant grass waving in a slight breeze a few hundred feet to our front and left flank. We were lying in the mud but not in any water. We had one starlight scope per squad, which was used constantly by the person on watch to look for enemy movement.

We just didn't want anything to happen that night, and we thought we had it made when Anderson said, "I think we have movement." "There's something out there," he kept saying over and over while I woke the rest of the squad. We all started taking turns looking through the starlight scope to see if we could pick up any enemy movement while Anderson and I kept saying, "This can't be happening, not tonight of all nights!"

To top it all off—and you couldn't put this in a comic strip—the "fuck you" lizards started up and began playing with our minds. We both lost it a little. The lizards start out, "foc quuu, foc quu, foc qu, fuc qu," and before long you start to think there's someone in front of you going "fuck you, fuck you!" Before panic completely overwhelmed us, our squad leader decided to call up the other ambush site about thirty feet from us and ask if we could join up with them. They had a better view and said they couldn't see any movement. We joined up with them after crawling through the mud. They did have a better view, and with two starlight scopes we could easily spot any movement and we didn't have to put up with any fuck you lizards.

The night turned out to be uneventful, to our relief. We both stayed up for the rest of the night, and I don't know if it was the possibility of blowing a bush on the enemy or thinking about home. It seemed like a GI Joe episode every day and every night, because these situations would play out with everyone in our platoon on many occasions. Nothing changes.

Other GIs would have the same experience with girlfriends or worse yet, wives. It was so difficult for them that many of us as squad members kept a close eye on them. It took a toll on grunts, and it wasn't always out in the field. It was when they got back to base or in a stand-down area after getting a letter from home.

In all cases, I felt lucky, but the one thing that really got to me in the long run was the picture in my head of myself and the other troops. We all looked like GI Joe and his buddies during WWII, dirty, grizzled, ragged, drawn, fatigued, living in a hole...I began to feel like I had been in Vietnam for so long, that I'd been born there.

I had lost track of something. Home was a figment of my imagination. It didn't exist anymore and this was to be my life until I was KIA...I would disappear and simply be replaced. We literally lived in the mud, in mud holes, in rotted jungle swamps. Our clothes were rotted, our feet were rotted, we'd lost all sense of smell, and we couldn't take our boots off anymore because our feet would swell up and we wouldn't be able to get them back on. Every night in our nighttime ambush site, when I wasn't on watch, I would wrap myself up in my poncho, throw my helmet in the mud, lie down in the mud, squirm and wiggle a little to get comfortable, lay my head in my helmet, and look at the stars. The one thing you could always count on, if only for a few hours, was watching a multitude of falling stars. It was incredible!

It would rain and rain on and off all night every night as I slowly sank in the mud. I would lay on my side and pull my poncho hood over my head, keeping my right ear inside my helmet and leaving an opening to look out so when it rained I could still try to sleep. The bad thing about that was when it rained hard, it would splash mud into my face, and if it quit before morning and had a chance to dry a little, I would wake up with my mouth and eyes cemented shut and I'd have these little mud breathing tubes sticking out of my nostrils. Opening my mouth wasn't so bad, but it was difficult opening my eyes. My eye lashes acted like re-bar in concrete. Water made it worse; it turned my whole face into a wet ball of mud. Once I was woken up with someone whispering "g _ _ ks" in my ear, which meant we were about to blow a bush, but my eyes were cemented shut! That does spook a guy.

Your clothes and gear can only get so dirty before turning into a thin layer of stiff mud. There was some relief if we got to an area with old bomb craters. They were filled with water that was green but wet. We would jump in, clothes and all, and it felt good to get somewhat clean. We could turn the water gray, and when we got out, we would feel lighter and our clothes would be almost green again.

Holidays were traditions that were celebrated by GI Joe and his buddies. We were served hot—or at least warm—food once and had a religious service twice while in the field. That was only when we happened to be off base for a very long period of time. We had Thanksgiving in the field with all the fixings, which was a mess, but the turkey was fantastic. We gorged ourselves on turkey and really good bread, then we ate turkey sandwiches while the chaplain held services. It was good food for the soul. We had communion and the whole bit. I didn't know what kind of service it was, I didn't ask, and I didn't care. The chaplain took the time to talk to each of us individually, and when he left, everyone went silent. It stayed that way while each of us found a spot to be by ourselves.

During these times, I would envision everyone going to church back home. We were, as usual, pretty filthy, but in my

Christmas 1969

mind I could see all the young ladies dressed to the hilt, all clean and foxy looking. I could see young wives, young girls, and young mothers with children all dressed up with their hair combed. Some little girls had decorations in their hair. The men were all dressed up in their shining suits, probably just back from the cleaners, all pressed. Their shoes were clean and polished, and they were probably wearing underwear, socks, and a belt. To this day, especially at Easter or Christmas, these thoughts come flooding back. I look at all the people and remember how it was.

13

PINNED

───────────────

DURING MY ENTIRE TIME in the field, there were only three or four times that our whole battalion was in a defensive position overnight. The one I really remember is the one in which my company, along with other companies, were pinned down for three days.

We were in the field and it was mid-afternoon when we got word that helicopters were en route to pick us up and we would be inserted as reinforcements for a marine unit in the middle of a firefight. We were to be inserted one click (kilometer) behind them and move in on line to provide direct support. It was a hot LZ, but we didn't get hit with any small arms fire. It seemed strangely quiet as we slowly moved in—no artillery, no airstrikes, and no sign of a firefight.

We made it to the area where we expected to find marines in a firefight, but there was no one in sight. Instead we found equipment. It looked like some outfit had been in the field, equipped to the max, got into a firefight, and ran. We found gas masks lying everywhere, which we never carried, empty ammo cans, loose M16 ammo, small belts of M60 ammo with eight-ten rounds, tubes of gun oil, clothes, helmets, towels, detonation cord, c-rations, backpacks, etc. This is something we knew never to do; I still get upset just thinking about it. The enemy could use all of that against us—ammo cans, backpacks, and clothes could all be used for booby traps; M16 ammo could be used in the AK47s the enemy carried. Right then, I hated the marines! These troops had no regard for others.

We policed the area thoroughly and sent out several recon squads for any sign of the marines (pounding their chests in bravado) and to determine the situation. Would we find more of the same? Were there enemy elements in the area and were there any marines still around? We held the position for the rest of the day and night until we got a sit rep (situation report) from aerial recon of possible enemy movement.

I never saw another marine nor did I ever want to after that ordeal. We were pulled out again, as choppers were coming and two other companies were in a firefight with fortified NVA. Not only were we going in, our whole battalion would be inserted, including the rest of Alpha Company along with Bravo Company, Charlie Company, Charlie Rangers Company, Delta Company, and our Special Forces Operations Platoon. We figured that the marines may have gotten tangled up with a forward element of this same NVA force and ran.

After being picked up, we landed and moved in a line, putting down a lot of firepower and strategically moving closer and closer to the enemy, one platoon at a time. Helicopter gunships and heavily armored planes called "snoopy" and "puff" (after Puff the Magic Dragon) were making rocket runs and then pulling off while heavy 155 artillery pounded the area. After that, the Loach observation choppers went in, and the fun started. A Loach went down and crashed about fifty yards in front of us. The pilots were out and okay when more gunships came, trying to secure the area with their mini-guns. I was putting down a heavy field of fire, giving the two pilots a chance to make a dash for it.

They blew by us at full speed and did a nice in-stride hurdle over the dike we were laying behind, keeping right on trucking out of there. The pilots had left everything in their chopper in order to be as light and fast as possible. Not only did they leave all their gear and small weapons, they had a mini-gun mounted on their chopper. We needed to get to it and retrieve everything we could, then blow up the radios. My platoon leader, 2-6, wanted me to move about a hundred feet to my left to put me on a machine gun nest. One ammo bearer and I made our way to a good position, where we were not exposed and 2-6 and 2-4 could direct my fire. My ammo bearers and I always had an agreement. They didn't want to be too close to me and I didn't want them moving around me. They would normally dump all their ammo, belt it all together, and move away.

I had already burned through half my ammo by the time I got into position. My ammo bearer belted up what he had for ammo and moved about ten feet to my right. 2-6 thought I had taken out that gun nest, but I didn't think so. In the process of putting down a lot of firepower with an M60, you give away your position because you're shooting a tracer every five rounds as well as cutting down all the grass in your fire lane. It was likely I'd receive return fire if I stuck around too long, which is what happened.

About that time F-4 fighter bombers were swooping down all around us. My ammo bearer pointed out one F-4 that was coming in on our right and he shouted, "He hit his pickle button!"This meant he was dropping bombs like napalm, clusters bombs, or bunker busters, which look like pickles. A second F-4 had dropped down behind the first, laying down an air strike right in front of us, and then a third F-4 came down and swooped in behind him, but did not drop any ordinance.

He came in from our right and flew past us, then banked to his left, flanking our left, then banked another left, so he was coming straight up our rear! I was lying on my stomach, shouldering my M60, but I kept my eyes on this F-4 as he was banking into his first left turn. I wasn't watching him when he banked again, but my ammo bearer was. He was lying on his back when he shouted at me, saying, "I think he's on a bombing run." I rolled over on my back. He was at least several thousand feet straight behind us and still banking his jet when he turned—then he was coming right up our 180 when he released two bombs. I saw them release and separate from under each wing, and I remember lifting my hands. I looked at my ammo bearer and he was doing the same thing...they were coming straight at us...couldn't miss.

My life didn't flash before my eyes like they say, but I figured I had ten, eleven, maybe twelve seconds at best to live. Strange as it was, I was somewhat calm...I guess since I didn't have any choice. I wondered where my guardian was, and then he said, "I'm right here." He was calm.

In those few seconds, I knew how it was going to happen and it was going to be instant—red slush. It looked like each bomb was right on target and I could easily see all four fins on the one that was coming right at me fast and true. I could see it barely moved from side to side as it slowly floated down right at me...and right over my head!

It all happened so fast I didn't see where it landed, but it exploded right away. I felt the full concussion and then the next thing I knew, I was suspended in time. It was like I was floating along in mid-air with these huge globs of mud and chunks of grass, along with my ammo bearer just a few feet away, also floating. All of a sudden I could feel myself falling. There were more huge globs of mud suspended above my head, about to fall, and when they did, both of us were buried. It weighed a ton—we were buried in mud, but still alive. After what seemed like eternity, my ammo bearer was the first to say something—"Hell, that wasn't even close!" Actually, they did hit close, but it felt even closer than it was.

The first squad, 2-1, dug us out of the mud and drug our butts out of there. Our whole platoon hooked up with the rest of our company. We stayed in that position for the next several days, hitting the battlefield with constant artillery, mortar, and air strikes. We could never get beyond a certain point where we kept getting pinned down. At night we would hold our center position and the outer flanks would fall back into a huge horseshoe-shaped defensive position. We continued with heavy bombardment all day and all night, but the enemy was dug in with a series of tunnels.

The second day someone was killed again in either Bravo or Charlie Company and more were wounded. They got their wounded out, but they couldn't reach their point man who had been killed. They set up as close as they could, but this time just couldn't move without getting hit with heavy machine gun fire. No one in my platoon knew the guy that was KIA, though we knew a couple of the guys that were wounded. We also knew they would somehow get their man out.

We were told they left him out overnight but stayed in position where they could always see him. We set up the same way we always did, in our nighttime defensive position; only this time artillery kept shooting flares up all night. It was about three o'clock in the morning when all hell broke loose. We had incoming mortars upon mortars and RPG fire. Then, just like that, it all quit. We figured it was their way of saying good-bye. Sure enough, the next morning everything was quiet.

The dead point man was dusted off along with more wounded from the mortar barrage and one of our guys from the first platoon with several broken fingers. Our company swept the battlefield until about three hundred feet in front of our original location, where we found a bunker system. We held that position until two other companies were able to sweep toward us and join up.

We didn't find anything in our sweep, nor did the other companies, except for some body parts. You couldn't tell what was there because it was like a soft-plowed field with small clumps of shredded grass and bits and pieces of trees and brush scattered about. We were close to the Cambodian border, where we suspected the enemy was watching us. We would leave the area and some day we would be back to do it all over again.

Our 2-1 squad had been able to retrieve that mini-gun and all the ammo and gear from the crashed Loach helicopter a few days earlier. They blew up the radios and electronics with incendiary grenades. There were additional helicopters that were shot down and crashed, because as we were getting ready to leave, there was about a half-dozen other choppers in the air hauling a damaged helicopter strapped under them, including the Loach that went down in front of us.

As we started to move out I was in deep thought, and it was then that I whispered to my inner sidekick, "So what do you think?" All I got back was a "grunt" for a grunt.

14

RIVER PATROL

PART OF OUR WEEKLY combat missions was doing patrols for the navy stationed at a supply base at Ben Luc on the Ben Luc River. There was a bridge spanning this river, which was part of Highway 1 that the U.S. government built. This bridge was referred to by some as "Y Bridge." It had been blown up by the Viet Cong several times. The navy patrolled the river constantly with their swift boats and gun boats, but it was our job to patrol the inner banks. We did this on a weekly basis. We both looked forward to and yet dreaded it every Thursday night. It was a hairy operation for the most part, but then again, it was a break for us, too.

Our job was to ride on boats called "Tango boats" up and down the river. We would move in a pack of five or six Tango boats, and if there was any activity, movement, or if something just didn't seem right, we would turn the boats and ram them through the vegetation onto shore, then would bail off—all at night. We worked off these Tango boats from sundown till around midnight or one o'clock in the morning.

It was totally uncomfortable riding on these boats. They were made of fiberglass and could not withstand any kind of attack from small arms, machine gun fire, or RPG assault. Riding on a Tango boat offered absolutely zero protection and we felt like sitting ducks. If a boat got hit by an RPG round, there was an eighty percent chance it would sink like a rock. If a Tango boat got hit, those driving it would take off as fast as they could, and, if at all possible, ram it up on shore or a mud bank before it could sink.

As they rammed these boats through the jungle vegetation, we would jump off and land in mud up to our waists and water up to our chests. We would be much lighter than usual and we could easily get ourselves out. My ammo bearers carried only five one-hundred-round belts of ammo each, besides their M16 and ammo. I had one belt rolled up in an assault bay attached to the side of my M60 and carried the other belts on my other shoulder. If we came into contact with the enemy, we could count on the navy to come in and cut loose with their swift boats and gun boats. Our favorite gun boat was named "Birth Control." A gun boat looked like one big pontoon boat with a flat roof and canvas curtains all the way around. Behind these curtains was every kind of armament you could think of. Massachusetts Senator John Kerry and his combat unit rode the swift boats and gun boats that supported the 9th Infantry Division.

We would move in on land maybe a few hundred feet and watch for anything and everything. Then we'd sit tight for awhile. We would call in artillery to shoot some flares in the background, allowing us to see any possible enemy movement silhouetted. The hairy part of this was that if there was any fighting, it was in the dark. This happened a lot. The one good thing was that if we got into any kind of a firefight, they were a ways off.

Moving in the dark was beyond scary, nerve-wracking, and hair-raising. Our contact with the enemy was never more than small skirmishes, hit and run. The hit part wasn't as bad as the run. When you were on the move, you couldn't see your hand in front of you. Many times we would move on the dikes rather than navigate the deep mud, but that meant the risk of booby traps, even though many of those areas were populated. What made things over-the-top scary was when we were in a small skirmish and needed to move, but it was pouring rain, pitch black, and there were family hooches with water buffalo in the area.

We had lots of trouble with animals when we were on the move. Many times we ran across the nastiest critters alive—fire ants. If there were snakes, you couldn't see or hear them, but you knew damn quick if anyone stepped on one. But the absolute worst, as far as I was concerned, was the water buffalo.

First off, they hated GIs. It's like having a family pet that doesn't like strangers. Some of the guys thought they could smell us, but I don't know about that. I do know they could strike the fear of God into you. The worst for me was one time when everything that could go wrong went wrong. We had been in a small skirmish when we blew a bush and made a sweep of our fire zone while artillery provided flares to help us see. Once that stopped, everything went black and we needed to move to a different location. It started pouring rain. We knew enemy VC were in the area and we were trying to navigate a small dike as quietly as possible. Guys were slipping and falling off the dike, and we were making way too much noise. They all needed help getting back on their feet, so guys were talking, sometimes pretty loud. Many of guys that were trying to help ended up being dragged down as well.

This was all happening close to an area that had water buffalo. I don't know if they were in a pen, which is usually the case, or if they were tied out in a rice paddy, but they started to snort, bellow, and paw. We heard somebody in a low voice say something in Vietnamese that sounded like "Nay, nay." Don't know if that meant stop or charge! More guys were sliding off the dike, including myself, and some started shooting towards where they thought the water buffalo were.

That scared the holy hell out of us because we didn't know what was being fired upon. All you see was a muzzle flash, but it was impossible to tell if it was from our own side or from somebody else. More guys started shooting and then more and soon it was nothing more than panic fire. By this time, everyone had either slid or jumped off that damn dike, and we just held our positions until we had a chance to settle down.

I don't know what happened to the water buffalo but I never heard another sound out of them. That was perfectly fine with me. We waited for artillery flares for background light and then the Tango boats started shooting up flares so we could find our way out. We were all happy to get on that boat, and we were then just hoping to make it back to the navy yard without the boat getting hit.

The positive thing about river ambushes was we weren't out all night. We could stand down for the rest of the night in the naval yard where we had warm water to clean up, and the mess hall was open twenty-four hours a day. We would use the warm showers and change our clothes. The other big deal was they had flushing toilets. We could also take off our boots and wear a one-size-fits-all navy deck shoe and try to dry our feet as much as possible, which felt fantastic.

Our next stop would be the mess hall, which is a misnomer— it should be called The Naval Restaurant and Supper Club. We could have steak and eggs to order—real eggs—with real milk, real potatoes, jams, jellies, and donuts. There was any kind of cold cut meat you could think of and real cheese. There were all kinds of salads with real salad dressing. You could have a burger for breakfast if you wanted, or even fried chicken. And you could have the most wonderful food in Vietnam—ice cream, beautiful ice cream, twenty-four hours a day!

This kind of food was a far cry from what we were used to. Normally, whenever we got the chance and we were close to a village, if we could stand the smell, we stopped at the village market. We would trade our C-rations (C's) for their native soup, which was really good. It had fresh garden vegetables and homemade noodles. The only downside, for a few us, was when we ended up sick and in the hospital.

Another time, a few of us were at a food stand that was serving something that looked like an apple turnover and smelled really good. It was wrapped in nicely browned bread dough, whatever it was. Although we were normally skeptical of everything we found in the market, these things looked good. We all wanted someone else to go first, so we could see what happened to them. Before one of us could volunteer, our tiger scout, Rup, rushed over and said, "No can do, no can do, number 10 thou... same same rat meat!" To this day I can't get close to an apple turnover.

Some time later, when we were in the field and standing down on a "hard-spot," we were unexpectedly lined up for feet inspections. Twenty-eight of us in Alpha Company alone were pulled off line until our feet recovered. They flew us all back to battalion HQ to receive immediate care. The doctors treated our feet and told us to take it easy, not to get our feet wet, and to eat well. So we did just that.

It was always easy to go down to the motor pool and grab a duce and half truck, a pickup, or a couple of jeeps. They didn't have keys in them, just an on-off switch, so off to Ben Luc we would go. The first vehicles out of the gate in the morning would be the mine sweepers clearing the road from HQ to Highway 1. There were a few times we were following them out the gate in the morning, on our way to have breakfast at the naval compound. Sometimes we would go later and have steak and mashed potatoes with gravy. They always had the best bread with real butter.

Back at Ben Luc, we would stand down for the rest of the night and also for a good part of the next day. Trucks would start to pull in about one o'clock in the afternoon and from there we would head back out to the field. We ate well and as often as we could. Some of the guys would take more showers and sometimes they would find the soft blue cotton pajamas used by a lot of the naval guys in the infirmary. It was something we actually looked forward to, although with a little apprehension. I would always think about the first part of going out on boats on ambush patrol and I know so did everyone else because no one would talk. We would all try to be focused. No one liked riding on those damn plastic bathtubs constantly being afraid of eating an RPG round or taking a direct hit from a rocket.

I needed a break from all the rain and the mud. It was getting to the point where I thought I couldn't take it anymore. As I may have mentioned before, the monsoons started in June, just when I got there, and lasted for months on end. I don't how long it had been when I really hit a low point, but it had been quite awhile.

There was a period of time when I was always in the mud and water, either working on the Tango boats or on patrol. I started thinking—I don't know if I was dreaming or wide awake—about how nice it would be if I came across a 4' by 4' "outhouse" to sleep in. Even if I was dreaming, I was bartering with whoever would listen. How much would it cost? What would I need to give up to have a measly little outhouse to crawl into?

I thought of how I could curl up, just small enough to lay on the wood floor, and how comfortable it would be and how nice it would be to have a roof over my head. I thought about how I could position myself so I could watch for enemy movement out of the door and how I could adjust myself if the rain came in.

Later on in life, whenever Marcia and I would talk about doing something to our house, I would remember this. I always said I didn't need much, remembering how much a little would have meant a lot to me...but then again it's all relative.

15

HANG FIRE

SEPTEMBER 7, 1969, STARTED out as usual. We were on patrol in an area southwest of Saigon, in Long An Province—an area we called "The Pineapple." This was a major infiltration zone with a lot of enemy activity. We were in a company-size unit moving on a fairly decent road, small but high and dry. Delta Company was about two clicks to our right flank and was getting hit with sporadic AK-47 fire from their left flank, which didn't make any sense. Why were they getting fired upon while we weren't? We weren't spared for long. As we moved in single file down this road, we noticed enemy movement between us and Delta Company. That's when we came under fire.

We weren't being hit with direct fire; instead, they sprayed us with automatic gun fire back and forth from left to right. It seemed like they just wanted to pin us down. We took cover behind a dike that was to the right side of this small road, then saw enemy movement closing in. We put down a heavy field of fire and then my squad was able to maneuver our position slightly to the left. Still, we came under more direct fire.

My platoon swept forward and ran into enemy KIA. The

one my squad came across was definitely VC, but was a little unusual—he wore the telltale black pajamas, but they looked shiny and new and he was older. We found ammo casings around him but no weapon, and his body wasn't booby-trapped. With this information from our squad and similar findings from the others, our CO thought maybe we had gotten tangled up with a forward element of a sizable VC or NVA unit infiltrating this area.

We moved back between the small road and dike, and were then able to slowly make our way forward another one hundred yards to where the road turned into a small path. Two inhabited family hooches were located there, probably fifty feet apart. There we set up security, and two more companies were called in. They were on their way in helicopters, along with more ammo and supplies.

My ammo bearers and I positioned ourselves just to the right of the first hooch, where we had a good field of vision. I started to put down small bursts of M60 fire to help secure the area. Helicopters were coming in five at a time, landing with their door gunners blazing away, because we had popped red smoke grenades indicating a hot LZ.

As I was firing my M60, there was an explosion very close to me, a flare that was hit by a bullet or shrapnel and exploded. At first I didn't realize I was hit in my right leg...and bleeding badly. Then my lower leg began to sting and felt very hot. I didn't know to what extent I was hit or if I even still had a leg. It happened so fast. I was slowly starting to get some more feeling back when the pain hit. Everyone around me had scattered in the chaos, thinking there would be more incoming fire, but

Recon — I'm still carrying the M60

when it settled down a bit, we realized that it was probably a "hang fire"—the kind of explosion caused when ammo is fired or hit by something, but doesn't detonate right away. Then when you least expect it, the damn thing explodes.

I had a hole in my leg about the size of a quarter, right at the boot line. Our medic, Doc Bailey, got right on it to stop the bleeding. Doc Bailey, my platoon sergeant, and several others put me on a departing helicopter still on the ground, rather than dispatch a dustoff Red Cross chopper. I don't remember a whole lot but I do remember the ride back to a field hospital.

Chopper pilots are crazy, no doubt about it! I was wounded, but I thought it was the helicopter ride that would kill me. They flew no more than five feet off the ground, going what I swear was about a hundred miles an hour. They would fly right over the top of a water buffalo working in a rice paddy, spooking it so it would take off, dragging the poor farmer behind. They would swoop over the top of hooches, scattering the palm branches that made up their roofs. I was sitting on the floor of the chopper, and of course there were no doors. I wedged my one good leg against the left pilot seat and hung on for dear life. I remember shouting "Okay Okay," not to invoke my inner guardian, but to let the pilots know I didn't want to die while they were doing aerial acrobatics. The pilots were having a good time. I soon heard from my sidekick...he was yelling "hee yeah!" and apparently having a great time.

In the end they got me to the field hospital in one piece. I thanked them over and over again. They just laughed, shook my hand, and wished me luck. The doctors immediately went to work. I remember them saying I was lucky—it could have been much worse.

The top of our jungle boots had a half-inch piece of leather stitched to the canvas around the top. That's where I was hit. My boot was mangled, but it took most of the impact. An inch higher and I wouldn't have gotten off so lightly. The surgeon told me he was doing a "particular kind of stitch" on my wound. There was only one light flickering behind him to help him see. When he was finished, he gave me pair of canvas shoes to wear and sent me off to a station bunker. I came down with a persistent infection but eventually returned to the field with my M60, as documented in my medical records. "Hee yeah"!!??

16

R & R

REST AND RELAXATION—R&R—comes in two flavors: in country and out. In country is optional and discretionary. Out of nowhere, I was told I had a three-day in-country R&R coming up in Vong Tao. I don't know what I did to earn it, but I didn't question it.

Vong Tao is located on the South China Sea and has some of the nicest beaches in the world, with white sugar sand and warm water. Three days was long enough to wear civilian clothes. In my case, I didn't have any civvies, but I borrowed some from the R&R center where I was staying. I must have looked like a clown wearing that plaid shirt and terrible pants, but they felt great. Better yet, I found some soft tennis shoes to wear. The bottoms of my feet were black—classic jungle rot—but oh man, those shoes felt good. With three days off, my feet would swell up and turn hard as a rock.

In-country R&R encourages the pursuit of the basic male instincts of wine, women, and song. There were a few other guys there from the 9th, so there was always someone to drink with, it seemed. There were girls everywhere. French

Oriental—owwww! The French army had been in Vietnam for years before we got there, so by the time we got there, the part French, part Vietnamese girls were twenty-four or twenty-five.

Everyone stayed in one hotel. It was not part of the R&R complex, but the military looked the other way, which made me a little uncomfortable. I asked about security and was told there would be no problems and no need to carry a weapon—don't worry, enjoy your stay! Not happy with that answer, I dug a little deeper and learned that not only was it an R&R center for us ground pounders and grunts, it was used by the VC and NVA in the surrounding villages. We weren't supposed to worry, since it was a "pacified" area! I was still on guard and sure as hell, I still had the crap scared out of me, with no weapon. Probably a good thing, though.

Grunts from other countries were staying at the center as well, including a dozen or so Aussies. One thing about the Aussies, they know how to drink! We tried to give them a run for their money...biiiiiig mistake. But man, did we party until I couldn't find my ass with both hands to save my ass. I don't have a clue how I made it back to my room.

Sometime that night, all hell broke loose with ground and air sirens, lights, and gunfire! I bailed out of my room. I ran into nine or ten other guys heading for a rear door. As we were making our mad dash, there were several rooms where a girl or in one case about four girls came bailing out. As we ran by this room, the door was open and we could see one of our Aussie buddies was sprawled out in the middle of the bed wearing lacy girls' underpants, obviously passed out. We didn't know what to think, but it didn't matter—we figured we were all dead anyway.

It was crazy. The girls ran in the opposite direction, and we couldn't understand a word they were saying. We blasted through the back door onto a balcony about twenty feet off the ground. The only way out was to go to the front of the building, which wasn't an option. There were a couple of four-foot knee walls on each corner of this balcony supporting the roof. We were able to scale these and make our way onto the roof. We laid down in a row, looking over the roof ridge, taking in all the action; it looked like a dang Chinese fire drill below. After staying frozen for awhile we began to wonder—if this was VC, wouldn't there be someone trying to hit back with some firepower? It was then we decided to find our way down and make a dash for the bar we had been at earlier.

At the edge of the roof, we found two small square structures with pieces of tin laying over them. We figured we could walk along one edge and shimmy down a wall to the ground. Two guys went first, stepping on one of the pieces of tin, which immediately gave in. Down they fell into a water cistern—we all began shouting, trying to get them out. More tin fell in, making more noise. We were finally able to yank them out, though not before they had been all cut up. After that plan failed, we knew we were all dead. There was no other way down!

As we crouched on this balcony, some of the girls who worked there came running towards us shouting, "Okay, okay, no sweat GI." We got up, planning to make a dash to a room with the help of these girls, where we could reinforce the door. Running back down the hall, we passed the door where the

Aussie was still passed out on the bed, laying there with the door wide open. We began to feel a little better, figuring there was a purpose behind all the action that we hadn't been told about.

As it turned out, it was the Vong Tao police making a raid on the hotel looking for Vietnamese girls who were not escorting a Vietnamese man but were with "someone else." Apparently these girls got sent to the monkey house, i.e. jail. I don't know what in the hell they were thinking!

It was a heck of a way to sober up, but I made sure I spent the next day recuperating, writing letters, laying in the shade, taking warm showers, wearing clean clothes—it was especially great to wear underwear again—and eating more ice cream. I knew I had to eat as much as I could, since who knew when I'd next see ice cream in Vietnam

Once my three-day R&R was over, it was back to the field. I still hadn't had my out-of-country, though. With each tour of duty, a GI is entitled to an out-of-country R&R, if they desire. Well, I DESIRED, and I also had a good ace in the hole. One of the guys in my squad from AIT was in charge of R&R for the 9th Division. I could get any location I wanted. If I wanted to go on two, I could do that too.

Australia was difficult to get because everyone wanted to go there, including the military brass. I wanted to go as well, but my girlfriend back home had a sister and brother-in-law in Hawaii and was insistent that I go there. My deployment had been trying for both of us already. It's hard to communicate while you're in the field.

It was difficult, but in the end I decided I wanted to see Australia, as it would probably be the only chance I had in my life to visit the country. Besides, I was lucky to get it. It turned out to be just what I was hoping it would be and much more. There were lots of humorous times.

Australia must have been ahead of its time in terms of the mini-skirt. Every girl wore one. No one in Vietnam knew anything about mini-skirts or that Australia was the leader in that fashion, so we were in for a surprise.

There must have been a hundred of us guys on the plane I flew in on, headed for the country down under. Everyone was whooping it up, happy and having a good time.

The plane landed on the tarmac and rolled up to an area where other planes were lined up. We were told to sit tight until we were cleared to unload. We watched the plane next to us as it was already unloading baggage and passengers were filing down the stairs. It looked to be fully unloaded of passengers when this girl stepped on the stair platform.

She had long blonde hair, a short, white fur coat with a big wide collar, and the shortest mini-skirt you've ever seen. She looked like a movie star! The entire plane load of guys went from crazy loud to absolute silence in a split second. Everyone was frozen in position, not daring to breathe.

The young woman then began to slowly walk down the stairs. This whole plane remained suspended in time for a good ten minutes until she finally disappeared into the terminal. It was the strangest thing. No one spoke and just looked straight ahead. We were cleared to exit the plane, and still no one would make a sound. We grabbed our things and slowly and meticulously made our way out.

There were about six of us who had flown out together from

brigade HQ, so we stayed together. We made it to our individual rooms, where we could shower—hot water—and then gathered in a big room where we were fitted for a suit. We could wear underwear, socks, and a belt too, without getting ring worm!

Our options for what to do next seemed limitless. If we wanted, we could even spend time on a ranch deep in the outback. We all decided to stay in downtown Sidney, called "Kings Cross," and take in the sights and sounds of the night life. It was certainly an eye opener and also a little disconcerting for a farm boy from Iowa.

In Australia, prostitution was legal and the communists had an active political party! Sidney had a huge park, which often featured young people spouting communist doctrine. That was so strange to me, because I thought the war was about fighting communism. The prostitutes were great, but not in the sense you may think. For the record, I did not partake, although I came away with a different perception of this industry. There was no sleaze factor associated with these gals. They were held in high regard. It wasn't considered a crime. They looked elegant and I swear they worked for the Chamber of Commerce! They acted like tour guides—are you having fun, have you seen this, so and so entertainer is in town, don't be afraid to ask any questions, don't miss our fabulous zoo, have you seen all our beautiful cathedrals and their magnificent gardens? They were right; the zoo was absolutely amazing, but the cathedrals and their surrounding gardens were really astonishing and I took some great pictures.

My first day was uneventful as we walked around downtown Sidney taking in the sights and sounds and hitting a few bars, of course. We bought more booze to take back to our hotel, who knows why. That evening, there was to be a harbor cruise up and down the Sidney harbor sponsored by the USO, including a band, girls, food, and drinks—wine, women, and song. It was like a throwback to the WWII USO events. It made us feel like we were almost human beings again. And I met a girl.

I wasn't about to make too much of it, thinking events like this were probably routine for many of the girls. She was quite attractive, as were they all. I just thought she was doing her job of trying to make some poor grunt happy.

We partied and she could really shake a leg with the best of them. We tore up the dance floor and everyone was having a good time. We partied till the wee hours of the morning until the band finally quit. We both had drunk way too much by then anyway. She got sick a couple of times over the side of the boat and I was so damn drunk I didn't think I could take another swallow. We made it back to my room where she got sick again and I must have passed out! I don't know what time it was when we both came to but she was in a panic because she had to call her folks just to let them know she was okay. Each day or night, she always had to check in with somebody.

As it turned out, she was really a pretty nice gal and we would spend the rest of my R&R together. We often went to the Sidney Motor Club, which was a night club/dinner club with lots of entertainment. We gave up on the heavy drinking, which was fine with the both of us; we just had a good time together.

We took in the Broadway production of *Hair*, which was absolutely amazing! The next night, we went to another night club to see Pat Paulson, a comedian, who was always running for president of the United States. Part of the Pat Paulson troupe were the Smothers Brothers, who we saw the following afternoon.

I spent my whole R&R with her. I even went to meet her parents! They were quite polite, though skeptical of me, but I didn't care. The family, including her brothers and sisters, lived in a nice moderate house with one car. They were religious, and originally from London, England.

When it was time for me to go, we agreed to write each other. She wanted me to try to secure another R&R. We wrote as much as we could and I really looked forward to her letters, even though I still had a girlfriend back home. Things were cooling off a little bit on that front anyway, all because I decided to go for R&R in Australia rather than Hawaii.

As we continued to write, I felt I was getting more and more emotionally involved, and began to feel somehow exposed, uncomfortable, like I was letting my guard down. It was at this point that something changed in me. I felt I couldn't let myself get too close. VA counselors say war vets make an emotional turn that stays with us for the rest of our lives, going into combat mode to protect ourselves.

I wrote and told her how I felt, that anything could happen to me and I didn't want to hurt anyone. We should move on with our lives. I told her it was great, beyond great, it was the best, but if we stopped writing to each other, no one would get hurt. It turned out to be pretty hard for both of us. I don't know, maybe it was a mistake.

I didn't know how to explain how I felt and I still don't, but Marcia, my wife, could always see it. If I got too close to something or someone, when I had to deal with feelings or emotions with family and friends, even with my two beautiful daughters, she would say, "Oops, there he goes, he's going to shut down now, he got too close, he's going into combat mode and I can see the curtain coming down." Or simply, "He's putting on his armor."

I think that's what the WWII guys were talking about. They had some regrets about not opening up more, and they would always encourage younger combat vets to do that. I don't know what to say...okay.

17

Nose-to-Nose Combat

NOSE TO NOSE DESCRIBES one measly day out of all the days of my life that has never gone away. It will seem a little unbelievable once you hear it. I lost another ammo bearer, and that along with the rest of the madness from that day left a permanent mark on me and would cause a lot of distress for Marcia.

Our platoon had been in the field for quite some time and was heading back to our base for a few days of stand down. The day in question was sunny, yet not too hot—just a nice morning when we walked through the front gate. As usual, we were exhausted, ragged, and dirty. As we were walking in, we passed the chapel and discovered it was a Sunday and a service was about to start.

Many of us thought what the heck. We dumped all our gear and equipment in a big pile in front of the chapel and went in. It didn't make any difference to me who was talking or what the service was about, because I never listened anyway. It felt like the only time and the only place where I could ever feel at peace—where, as I said, "I could close both eyes."

I told myself, "Mmmm...if I was to get killed now, it wouldn't be so bad." If the chapel took a direct hit from a mortar or rocket, at least I would be ready and it would be quick. The chapel was nothing more than a hooch-type structure with canvas sides, a palm-covered canvas roof, and a dirt floor with straw mats. The altar was a small wooden stand sitting on two shipping pallets. The congregation sat on rough-cut planks. It wasn't much, but it gave me a tremendous amount of comfort.

Just as services were ending and we were walking out, I remember looking at our pile of equipment, clothing, and gear and realizing that it was nothing but one big, stinking, wet, dirty pile of muck. I could actually see waves rising off the top. It wasn't raining as we walked back to our stand-down area. The sun felt great and we were actually able to walk on some dry patches of ground. We were anticipating how nice it would be to get a few days rest and to dry our feet a little.

It was not to be. Only a few hours later we got the call to saddle up. Choppers were on their way and we were going back out into the field as reinforcements in an area where there was heavy fighting. I remember I was so frustrated, just because I didn't want to get wet again. I had only been dry for a little over a half day and I just wanted to go hide. We saddled up with full gear and made our way to the chopper PZ (pick-up zone). Before long we were on our way to be inserted with two of our battalion companies next to a company from the 2/47th. We were to land one click (one thousand meters) to their front left flank behind an embedded enemy in a heavily wooded area. The plan was to be inserted quickly, spread out, and slowly sneak in and around a hooch area that bordered

Future Viet Cong

this wood line. We would have a clear line of sight for about three hundred feet in front of us.

The choppers were coming into their LZ, and as they started to flare, I was still thinking I didn't want to get wet and I didn't want to jump. I stood on the helicopter's landing skid, as I always did, with my M60 at the ready, looking for a dry spot. No luck. Damn, I can still see the water and myself jumping off that chopper, getting wet all over again, and I can especially remember how it aggravated me to no end.

As it got darker, we moved closer and closer to our target hooch area, planning to set up ambush sites behind these hooches that bordered the wood line. We looked for small dikes leading out from the hooches that trailed off into small clearings on the back side of the brush line where we could set out anti-personnel mines. Half of our squad set up an ambush position off the back corner of one of the hooches where a dike was located that led straight into the tree line. We sat quietly looking and listening for anything and everything that moved.

We were in a good spot behind that hooch. It gave us a black background that would make it hard for the enemy to spot us. We sat for some time before putting out any claymore mines and establishing our individual fire lanes. As we sat there, all of a sudden we began to hear a rushing sound. It was slowly moving our way, getting louder and louder.

Around this time, some of the guys had started setting out claymore mines. Whenever this was done, we would all maintain radio communication. The ambush position to our immediate left called in to alert us with the words "2-2, 2-4—out front—claymore," and we responded, "2-2—looking." The noise we were hearing was getting louder and louder and louder! It was almost deafening, like a freight train coming right at us. We had never heard anything like it before.

We realized what it was when a monster cloud burst moved over the huge area of trees and jungle in front of us, about to hit us head on. Just as this cloud burst was about to hit, I quickly got on my knees, straddling my M60 and our radio, and pulled my poncho over everything, providing a good cover. In a few minutes we got hit with a wall of water and wind we had never experienced before nor ever would again. The rest of my squad quickly ducked into the hooch behind us with our platoon leader and his RTO man, where they could dig out their ponchos.

I was half-sitting, half-straddling my M60, bracing myself with my left hand and holding the radio receiver in my right hand where I had it tucked under my poncho. I held the receiver against my left ear and peeked out under my poncho hood, continuing to keep an eye out for Bundy, who still might be out in front of me somewhere. There was lightening over us and I could see a silhouette of someone coming right at me. It was raining so hard I couldn't see who it was. As this person got a little closer, I saw that he was wearing a jungle hat and had a weapon slung across his front.

I blinked and thought, Bundy wears a helmet! In a split second, this person was right next to me. Just then, one of my ammo bearers came out the hooch door and this person immediately went down on one knee, so we were shoulder to shoulder. He was VC or NVA! I turned my head towards him when he turned his toward me. We were nose to nose, eyeball to eyeball—then all hell broke loose.

We both jumped up at the same time. I struggled to get the poncho off with the radio cord wrapped around my neck, realizing I'd be screwed if it came to hand-to-hand combat. As I tried to throw off my poncho, I hit his AK-47 and hit myself in the teeth. That dazed me a little, but as I was still trying to get that damn poncho off I shouted to my ammo bearer, "Shoot, shoot, shoot!" and he froze.

I never did get my poncho all the way off, but I was able to grab my M60 and let it run. The VC had disappeared, I don't know where to. To my chagrin, I had failed to notice that the other guys in my squad had left their M16s under my M60 so they wouldn't get wet before they ducked inside the hooch.

My ammo bearer told me later it looked like I was wrestling with someone and shouting, "Shoot, shoot," then saying, "Don't shoot, don't shoot!" We were lighting up the area and peppering the wood line but it was raining so hard we couldn't find or see anything.

About four or five hours later, in the early morning hours, we were hit. Our ambush site continued to hold our position facing the wood line in front of us and provided fire power to our left and right flanks. When we got hit, at our eight o'clock position, one of my ammo bearers and others moved to a different position. The brunt of the firefight was with several other ambush sites and it was intense. They blew all their claymore mines and had a heavy exchange of small arms fire, machine gun fire, and grenade launchers with red and green tracer rounds flying everywhere.

As it started to get a little light out, the fighting stopped and we could see how intense it had been. There was enemy KIA everywhere. No one in all our ambush sites was killed or wounded.

The rain stopped and artillery started pounding the wooded area near us, while there was a commotion going on behind us. Finally our RTO man went to investigate, and came back shortly with the scoop.

He said my ammo bearer had got his hair parted with a bullet and that he was a total basket case! No one believed him. Technically, we didn't think this could be done, but he said it was true. He saw it for himself. As we started to saddle up, my ammo bearer showed up to join the squad and we had to check it out. He had a part in his hair about three inches long where there was a red streak and a line of little hair stubble across his head. It's nothing to laugh about, but we couldn't believe our eyes. If there is such a thing as being "shell-shocked," he was it.

As we started to move out, we crossed the area where all the fighting had been. There were quite a few dead bodies. Some of them were lying across the paddy dikes we were moving on and we had to step over them. He couldn't do it—he froze at the site of an enemy KIA and was jumping all around to different positions as we moved.

We were scared he would shoot someone, he was so jumpy, so we started to keep an eye on him. If there was a sound or any quick movement, he would draw down on it with his M16. This spooked the hell out of everyone. We were scared he would draw on us and shoot. It was so bad we all thought that if our point man or anybody else would have to shoot for some reason, this guy would panic and open up with his M16 in that direction and shoot one of our own. We eventually tried to shelter this guy, for our own safety, until we could get him out of the field. Later, we heard he re-upped to serve four more years in the army, and by doing that, he was pulled off-line and shipped back to the states. I can still see his face and the fear in it. I would think about him often, later, hoping he was doing fine.

Looking back on the events of this day, I don't know if they were the cause of Marcia waking up in the middle of the night to find me up close and personal, eyeball to eyeball. She'd scream and run out of the bedroom, while I would just slither off the bed, and according to her, lay on the floor watching her with predatory eyes. It sure does scare the crap out of her until I snap out of it.

I must admit though, I've dealt with a lot of bad nights. The older you get, the worse they get. When it used to take one day to recover, now it seems like it takes three days just to catch my breath, for my chest to quick hurting, and to get what I call all the "snow" out of my head. On some bad nights, I'd chew up the inside of my mouth and bite my tongue so bad I'd have blood all over my face and pillow. The next day it would heal a bit and feel better, but I would worry I'd do it again the next night. Nothing hurts worse than biting your tongue in the same spot every night for a week! Even mouth guards didn't work, since I'd chew them up into a mess too. Sometimes I would think it was a "catch-22 thing." I could hardly believe it, but I eventually went to see a "dreams doctor" through the VA, which was extremely beneficial.

18

A Tough Loss

AS I MENTIONED EARLIER, there were five of us who had the same amount of time on line. One of them, Weyant, was my ammo bearer from the start. He had a four-year degree in education and was a teacher from Beacon, New York. He had been drafted, like the rest of us, and he was quite a character, to say the least.

One of the other guys was our point man, Anderson. He was a wiry sort of guy who was good at his job. Anderson had this amazing intuition, a sort of sixth sense. We would lose Anderson and later, Weyant, along with five others trying to rescue him.

I remember these losses were a triple hit for me because I had found out my younger brother, Corky, had been in a bad car accident back home. The only information I had was that he was in serious condition, and a passenger was in intensive care with serious injuries. When you heard things like this from home, it weighed on your mind a lot.

The day I got word of my brother, my platoon was on patrol in an area that was suspected of being another supply route. We were paralleling a small trail through a destroyed pineapple field into a heavily wooded area with several clearings. The trail disappeared in front of us under the canopy. Anderson was walking point as usual and was well off the trail when he hit a booby trap, which caused a good-size explosion. We heard him calling for a medic.

The rest of our squad quickly set up a machine gun nest for me and our "thump gunner" to secure the area and watch for anything that moved, to keep us from being ambushed. My ammo bearers off-loaded all their ammo, belted it together, and moved away. This helped them go from being heavily loaded to being light and fast. I had established a good field of vision for my M60 when some guys, including Weyant, went in after Anderson.

Soon there was another explosion, bigger than the first. Immediately after that explosion there was another. They had hit a "daisy chain!" The first platoon was coming up behind us and when they arrived, they took over my spot. Their point man took over my M60 and I took his shotgun. The rest of our squad started in after our guys. We had seven guys down. None were dead, but they were in bad shape. We were able to carry them out, following the same trail we'd come in on, trying to step in the footprints we'd made before so as not to set off any more traps. We piggybacked all seven guys out into what we thought was a safe clearing. Medics were doing what they could, as were the rest of us. Weyant was hurting; no question about it. Anderson was the worst. I can't remember much about the other five guys; they were new replacements and in a state of shock.

A dustoff chopper came in and myself, Addington, and Beck loaded up our two buddies, Anderson and Weyant. The wounded were put on stretchers, and we stacked them up inside the chopper, telling them they would be alright. Neither Anderson nor Weyant said a word.

Like I said before, "You don't say hello and you don't say good-bye." If you don't say hello, you don't have to say good-bye. Sometimes guys would say it's pretty hard to get killed if you're already dead and you just don't know it yet. I wondered if that's what Anderson and Weyant were thinking.

Addington, Beck, and I all thought that was the last we'd see of these two guys. They were hurt bad enough to be shipped back to the states. Losing another seven guys cut our platoon in half again. Those of us who were left gathered up our gear and pulled out. We stayed in the field for another two days and during that time, we never received word that anyone had died. So as far as we knew, everyone was still at the Ton Sun Nhut/Saigon hospital.

We made it in early to our stand-down area where Beck and I quickly cleaned up and decided to go AWOL, if there was such a thing in Vietnam, and travel to Saigon to see if we could find the hospital where Anderson and Weyant were. Addington was going to run decoy for us, if anyone asked where we were.

We hopped on a water truck heading for Saigon outside the front gate of the base. We had only MPC (military paper currency—we called it Monopoly money for its striking resemblance to the fake dollars from that game) and no weapons. All I carried was my dog tags and rosary around my neck—

neither of us had any form of ID. We made it to Saigon and hailed a taxi, which was nothing more than a fifty CC Honda with a bench mounted on the front tire. Passengers were basically the front bumper. We went flying through Saigon, more than once ready to bail off to save our necks. I think my sidekick GA was going "Hee yeah" again! We found out later that using these taxis was totally prohibited. But we didn't know that at the time.

We miraculously made it to the hospital and we were able to walk right in, no questions asked. We were right that they were there—or at least they both had been, and Weyant still was. Anderson was in worse shape and had already been shipped out to a hospital in Japan for more surgery.

We walked in on Weyant and there sat our CO, Captain Johnson, his driver, and our platoon leader Lt. Baker. We didn't say a word. Strangely enough, neither did they. I thought for sure we were cooked. We sat for a bit when they got up, gave Weyant their best wishes, and left. He didn't hear them because he didn't know "come here from sic' em." He was in a lot of pain and must have had hundreds of stitches. He looked as if he had been sliced and diced! I wouldn't learn the extent of the trouble his injuries caused him until some forty-three years later.

He wanted me to write a letter to his folks, which I did. I wrote and told them who I was, what Weyant did, and what happened to him. I tried as much as I could to describe what he looked like. I then wrote down a message from Weyant. It was tough for him, but he was able to write, "Love you all," and sign his name. He was dozing off when we slipped out.

We didn't say good-bye, but I left him a note that I would make sure his letter was sent and drew the peace sign.

We missed the water truck and spent the night in Saigon. That was a long night. It was also something to experience the night life! Beck and I wondered if there was really a war going on. We eventually made it back to our unit late the next day.

We never got a letter from any of our wounded to let us know how they were doing, except Anderson. It was the end of January, four months later, when we got a letter from him. He told us he had lots of plastic in him and that if he lit a cigarette, he would melt. He was kind of right; he had a plastic jugular vein in his neck. He said he lost half of so many things in his body, that he was half a man, but he also had a good outlook.

He was back at Walter Reed for more surgery but he did get a month leave over Christmas. During leave he got married, his wife was already pregnant, he bought a new Chevy Chevelle, and was hoping to start college. He was an amazing guy. I've heard from a lot of guys over the years and through a network of people found some others, but no one can find Anderson.

Finding Weyant wasn't easy either. It was at least twenty-five years after our last meeting in the hospital in Saigon before I tried to locate him. I started calling every Weyant I could find in Beacon, New York, and after a couple of tries, I got his parents. I gave them my name and they instantly knew who I was. We had quite a chat and they gave me his phone number. I called and talked to him for a bit, and it was like he had never heard of me. Strange, but no big deal—I could understand. I tried to call him again about three or four years later and couldn't reach him. I called his folks again and they gave me another number to call. This time I had the feeling they were in the dark about where Weyant was and what he was doing.

I called the number and got him. This time our conversation was a little better. I'm still not sure, but I think he had been married and divorced more than once. He said he was married and had an older adopted teenage son.

Over the last couple of years we've talked a few more times and it's certainly been better. The last time I talked to him, I mentioned writing that letter home for him while he was in the hospital, and he said, "Oh, that was you." That really surprised me, but it helped me understand how Weyant was dealing with life after Vietnam. He made the comment that there is no glory in war and no glory in life after Vietnam. He said we all come home dead, they just forgot to bury some of us. Then we have to start all over again.

I did think it was weird that he didn't remember me writing that letter. He told me he was in bad shape. I told him I knew that, that he had been in and out of consciousness, but still seemed alert enough to know what was going on. He then said he didn't know if I knew it or not, but he took a piece of shrapnel up his dick! I said, hell no, I didn't know that, but I didn't think it would have affected your memory! He said it was bad, bad, bad, when they went in and dug it out. I was laughing my head off on the phone, holding my own Schwartz at the same time, thinking how that must have hurt. I asked him, "Didn't they put you to sleep or something?" He said hell no. They tried to put his dick to sleep, but he said, "I don't think they go to sleep—it was just bad!"

The last time I talked with Weyant was when I attended my first combat unit reunion. Some of us called him from my hotel room and we got a good laugh out of him. I told him that if we all ever got together, the first thing he would have to do is to whip out this mangled appendage for us so we could check it out. We got him laughing and felt good about that. We felt he was doing...okay.

19

DON'T STOP

THERE WERE MANY TIMES while I was in the field that I thought my emotional brain was having a conversation with my spiritual brain. The spiritual side seemed to be doing all the directing. These thoughts gave me comfort, knowing that if I were to catch a bullet, I would be prepared. Not worrying about dying so much allowed me to think with more clarity, with no panic, and somehow it kept me safe. I was able to do my job and do what was right for my platoon.

One firefight has always stayed with me. The majority of our contact with the enemy was with small elements of Viet Cong. This was our mode of operation. The 9th Division was known to make contact with the VC on an almost daily basis. Other divisions made enemy contact more rarely, but when they did, it was with a sizeable NVA unit in a prolonged firefight.

Most of our area of operation was a huge region west of Saigon called the Plain of Reeds, cut in half by the BoBo Canal. It was a major infiltration route coming out of Cambodia in an area called Parrot's Beak. Commanders in the field wanted

Family Hooch – Plain of Reeds

to have a huge presence in this area, which they saw as a security risk to Saigon, with as few troops as possible.

The 5/60th would patrol this area. That meant a lot of Eagle Flights and air-cushion vehicles—ACVs. Many times, my squad would ride on both for a single search-and-destroy operation. We would be based right on the BoBo Canal, securing a spot for refueling, resupplies, and reinforcements. Many times, I would ride as a door gunner on an ACV, and my squad was on guard duty around BoBo.

Once, while I was riding as a door gunner, one of the other two ACVs was hit and damaged. It was midday when we ran square into a fortified NVA force at Parrot's Beak and came under heavy weapon fire. The ACV I was on and the other secured the third as it limped back to our hard spot on BoBo.

Our platoon was saddling up, waiting for the choppers, and my ammo bearers were waiting for me. The choppers picked us up and inserted us into an area that I thought might be in the proximity of where we were when we had encountered enemy fire with the ACVs. As we moved in, we were caught in the middle of a major battle. There were causalities and wounded all around us, including some from our platoon.

Our RTO operator was shot several times in both his legs, with the worst wound in the middle of his right upper thigh, pumping out a lot of blood. Dustoff choppers were in the area to evacuate the wounded and dead. The fighting had stopped where we were, so our squad quickly decided to move over and past where our wounded RTO man was. Since no one was shooting at us, and no one was on their right flank, we made it over and behind some small cover. We could see nothing moving. We were about one hundred and fifty feet from a wood line in front of us when we got word our guy was next in line to be picked up by one of the dustoff choppers.

A few of us who were carrying M60s made up our own special ammo belts for certain occasions. The standard ammo belts contained one hundred rounds and every fifth was a red tracer round. These belts were made so they could easily be clipped together for continuous firing.

I got the idea one night while watching Cobra gunships off in the distance open up with their mini-guns. They shot the same belted ammo as my M60 and at night it looked like a straight red line coming from the sky that was dancing all around. It looked quite daunting, with some even ricocheting back up in the air. I thought that had to have an extreme psychological effect for anyone on the receiving end. So I put together two ammo belts where every other round was a tracer round. I would carry one belt and one of my ammo bearers would carry the other.

When our platoon leader told us the chopper was coming to pick up our guy, I got ready to provide security by belting up with both special ammo belts. We watched the chopper swing around, coming straight at us. As he started to flare and set down, both door gunners opened up with their M60s. There was a small tree stump about six inches high a little ahead of me. As soon as the door gunners opened up, I popped up, sat my M60 on this stump, and started sweeping the wood line back and forth, peppering it with tracer fire from my special ammo belts.

As soon as I started this...and I don't know what to call it, maybe divine intervention, but as soon as I popped up I heard in my head, "Don't stop—you stop, you die...you stop, you die!"

The dustoff chopper had just sat down and I had made a couple of sweeps with my M60 when my ammo bearer on my right started shouting at me to shoot, shoot, shoot! All of a sudden I couldn't believe my eyes—clumps of grass were popping out of the ground and running everywhere in front of me, up and down this wood line. Then I heard again, "Don't stop—you stop, you die," so I started shouting back to my ammo bearers, "You shoot, you shoot, you shoot," and I just continued firing tracer rounds up and down the wood line and at anything that moved.

To this day I don't know why we weren't fired upon. We were shouting for the chopper carrying our wounded man and other wounded to get going, afraid it would take on small arms fire because if it did, they would have been slaughtered. I kept hearing over and over, "Don't stop—you stop, you die," while my ammo bearer clipped on more ammo and my barrel was getting hot. I always had a small towel folded up and tied on with shoestrings as padding for carrying the gun on my shoulder. The shoestrings and towel would catch on fire if my gun barrel got too hot. At that moment, it was red hot and everything was on fire.

In cases like that, you could have what they call a "cook-off." That was when the barrel got so hot, the bullets fired just from the heat of the barrel, without you pulling the trigger. If that happened, you just had to hang onto it until you ran out of ammo. I hadn't had that situation, yet, but I knew it was close when the chopper finally lifted off and went right over the top of the wood line with both door gunners still firing away. Those pilots and gunners had more guts than brains.

I finally thought everyone and everything was in the clear. There was still no return fire, so I slid back down behind some cover, rolled on my back, and heard the words, "That was dumb—you could have been hit and you would have been a hell of a lot of help." I figured I was just talking to myself, until I heard, "Yeah yeah, okay."

We moved back a few guys at a time, until our whole platoon had retreated a few hundred feet. Then F-4 fighters came in and started dropping pickles (napalm). It got real hot real quick. We started to move in and around, trying to sweep the area as much as we could, but there was napalm still stuck to the grass.

When napalm cools, it leaves a soft foam-like substance on the outer edges of the blast area and sticks to everything. Our clothes, most of time, were so thin and half-rotten, they would easily rip and tear. This was the case here when we started to move, and most of us burnt our legs. That is not fun. It only takes the slightest touch and you're cooked. I don't know what's worse—napalm or fire ants.

I don't remember the name of the RTO guy who was shot in the legs. I can still see him, but he's another one of many I wondered what happen to. I don't even know if he lost a leg or both. No one knew any of the guys that were KIA or wounded in the other companies.

I've heard people say that if you're hearing voices in your head you're verifiably insane. I've thought about that a lot, trying to figure it—or me—or him—or them out!

20

THAT DANG ROSARY

━━━━━━━━━━━

WHEN I DECIDED TO WEAR my First Communion rosary around my neck when I left for Vietnam, I didn't think it would take on a life of its own. My uncle Gene, who told me to have something that meant something, some expression of security, was a WWII vet, and his advice meant a lot to me. I was lucky enough, when I returned from Vietnam, to have the chance to thank him and tell him it had made a difference in my life. It was emotional.

As I mentioned earlier, that dang rosary caused me grief the very first night in country. I started out wearing it loose around my neck, along with my dog tags. However, we were issued a plastic outer coating for our dog tags so they didn't make noise. That may have helped a bit to keep that rosary intact, but still, it wasn't long before it started to take a beating. The wooden beads were soaked in sweat most of the time and the links were caked with mud. It broke on me a few times. It was easy to fix with my handy-dandy multi-tool P38 can opener. I noticed it was slowly getting weaker and weaker, though. As time went on I got the idea to tape it to my dog tags, which worked well, for awhile.

We "ground-pounders" or "grunts" carried everything with us. I would carry the M60 most of the time balanced on my right shoulder, several belts of ammo over my left shoulder, and my backpack, which didn't amount to much. It was mostly a frame where I would tie my C-rations, or "C's," lined up across it. We would stack cans of C's in a sock and tie them on. I would also carry an extra machine gun barrel inside a handy asbestos bag that was tied to a shoulder strap and frame. I had everything in there. My cigarettes, my army spoon, a bottle of Tabasco sauce wrapped in tape, insect repellent, gun oil, iodine tablets, packets of kool-aid, small pieces of fine wire, and parts of my rosary. It would break a lot and I would patch it together with small wire.

I mentioned earlier that we worked off navy boats every Thursday night and then had Friday morning to ourselves. Well, that was rosary-fixing day for me, and strangely enough, my gun team and a few others would sit around and watch.

The main body of that rosary, the part that circled my neck, hardly ever broke. There were some links between beads that looked like they'd been stretched to ten times their original size, but had never broken. If it did happen to break in that part, it was hard to fix, since there was such as small space between the beads. More often it would break at the part that hung down front, at the three-point connector or the cross or previously fixed wire connectors in between beads.

It didn't make any difference to me what it looked like in the end; the act of fixing it gave me a great deal of comfort and was especially calming. If anyone came across some fine wire, they would give it to me knowing what it was used for. Sometimes, if we were all standing down, a lot of us would sit around drinking a few beers, and while some were reading mail or writing a letter, I would patch my rosary. I always felt that rosary provided a degree of comfort for them, too.

After awhile, the three-point connector completely wore out. I kept wiring everything together in one big circle. That worked well, and if it broke, sometimes I could fix it on the go or throw any extra pieces in my barrel bag and wire together whatever was left. It would get pretty short sometimes.

Seemed like that dang rosary was always up to something, and by far the strangest incident involved my encounter with Miss June or July, a centerfold Playboy bunny.

We were on Eagle Flights one day, being constantly dropped off to patrol an area and then shortly after picked up again. We did this four of five times that day. The chopper pilots were really a good bunch of guys. Sometimes they would have Cokes for us if it was the last PZ of the day. On this day, every time they picked us up, they told us about a USO troupe that was flying around visiting different bases. After our last PZ of the day, when we were heading back to base, they told us they thought we would have two Playboy bunnies, one professional model, and two professional boxers waiting for us.

When we returned to base, the choppers dropped us off outside our base perimeter and we humped it in from there. As soon as we made it to our bunker, many dropped their gear and took off for the "square," which was just a small concrete pad situated between the mess hall, a small ceremonial stage, and battalion HQ.

A couple of guys staying in our bunker said the water truck had just arrived and pumped up five hundred gallons of water into the holding tank above the showers. A bunch of us decided to clean up, take a shower, and change into clean fatigues. Most of the guys that had taken off right away for the square were on their way back, and they told us there was just one Playboy bunny and one professional boxer.

The boxer was a black fellow and they said the blacks were being disruptive, which is what they did a lot back then. At the time, there was a lot of protesting by the black troops, saying that the Vietnam War was not their war. There was much racial separation, rampant drug abuse, and base violence, and many blacks refused to go to the field. The guys returning from the square said as they were starting to leave, many of the blacks were leaving also, which is what their objective was. The rest of us decided to go see what was going on.

When we reached the square, there were maybe a couple dozen blacks around the black boxer doing their prolonged, black brother handshakes. When they were done with one, they'd start all over again—seemed kind of crazy. The Playboy bunny was standing all by herself with one photographer. She looked bewildered, like she was wondering what the hell she was doing there.

This is a little derogatory, but I said to myself, "Wow, she's the first round-eyed I've seen in months!" She was quite petite—you wouldn't have thought she was a centerfold

Playboy bunny. She looked like a lot of American girls, only with no makeup on whatsoever. She was a strawberry blonde having a bad hair day, sweating, dirty, dusty, and with a look in her eyes saying, "Get me the hell out of here, I just want to take a bath!" I thought she was the prettiest thing I had seen in a long time.

I walked up to her, and in a very nice, soft-spoken, gracious voice she said, "How are you?" I don't know what she must have thought of me, because I just stood there looking at her and I couldn't squeeze a word out for the life of me, no matter how hard I tried! She asked me what my name was and I think I did manage a croak or two. Then I grabbed my dog tags and pointed at my name. My God, looking back I have to laugh. It was then that she noticed my rosary. She reached out and took both my dog tags and rosary in her hand and just looked at me with the most interested look I've ever seen.

She continued to try and make conversation. Where are you from, where is home, do you have a girlfriend back home, are you getting letters in the mail, have you been wounded or sick, are you a short-timer? Still not getting anything, she smiled at me and grabbed my arm again and asked me how long had I been there?

Finally, I got a few words out and she asked me if I would like to have my picture taken with her. Sure, I said. I moved closer to her, and I could smell her perfume or her hair spray. Then I must have made a sound, like "Mmmmmm." She looked at me, smiled, and asked what I'd said. I said I liked her perfume and that I hadn't smelled anything like it for a long, long time. She then said, there's no one else in line, would you like a soda? "A soda?" I asked, and then she said, "A Coke or something?" I thanked her and said that my platoon had just returned from the field and I had to go be with them.

At that she asked if maybe instead I'd like to have a beer. It might be a little warm, but she could have the photographer get a couple for us. Again I thanked her and said I should be going, and she did something I'll never forget and still get emotional about. She was probably just doing her job, trying to make me feel good for a little while. She reached up and laid her hand on my chest over my dog tags and rosary and said, "You take care of yourself, be safe, and make sure you make it home. Okay? We want you."

We smiled at each other, then I looked down at the ground and left. I made it around the corner of the square before I started to think, "What am I doing?"

I only had about another fifty feet to go before I came to a road, just across from which was my bunker. I stopped. This road was nothing but a muddy, sloppy, stinking mess. I stood there and asked myself, "Why the hell do I need to be with these assholes when I could be with her?" I stood there staring at all that damn mud, not wanting to take one step. Then I thought, "Oh God, she must think I'm queer!" Then I asked myself, "Oh my God, am I turning queer?" I turned around and went back. As I neared the square, I could see her photographer, but she was nowhere in sight. I felt then that I had either gained something or lost something. I still don't know.

Another time, a bunch of us from our platoon went to the chapel for some sort of service. We were all sitting near, but not too near each other. I was sitting on the second plank from the back when two young Vietnamese women came in and sat down on the same plank, down at the end. I didn't really notice them.

I was sitting there like a lump on a stump, daydreaming and not paying attention to what was going on or being said. Like I said before, it was the only place where I felt I could close both eyes. A buddy behind me poked me and pointed at the two young girls. It was not an unusual sight, because there were a lot of Vietnamese workers that held all kinds of jobs on base. I looked over at them and they were smiling at me.

My buddies around me told me to say hello. I still didn't know what was going on, so I looked at them and shrugged my shoulders. The one closest to me made a gesture under her neck to show she noticed I was wearing a rosary. We just smiled at each other. She was a pretty gal. I think she was part French, part Oriental, which I think are the most beautiful women in the world. She had on the traditional long white robe with the standard full-length white shawl. She had long, shiny black hair halfway down to her waist...I was "beaucoup dinky dau." During the service we got to hold hands during prayer. That was a buzz!

I guessed she was looking at me because she thought it strange that I had a rosary around my neck. After services my buddies were egging me on, saying, "Go get her, Ready Freddy." I asked if they thought she would go have a beer with me after chapel services...I didn't think so! They all laughed and said maybe not, but she sure was smiling at me. I told them maybe she just wanted to go somewhere to say the rosary with me!!??

This next story about that dang rosary may still be alive and well to this day. Probably the more it's told, the more it gets stretched.

If we were moving a long distance—"humping the paddies"—it never took long for the trash talk to start. One of the first ones to start was always Weyant, my trusty ammo bearer. He would start on me to see how far he could get before I would blow my stack. He always walked behind me, and behind him came Hester.

Hester was a big black dude who always had a smile on his face, with your standard gold front tooth. He was quite a character. He carried the M79 thump gun, which everyone is probably familiar with because it's the weapon shown in movies when they pump tear gas into a building. It holds just one shell that's a little bigger than a Hostess Twinkie, which is pretty big. They carried it with the breech broke open and laid their thumb on the grenade to secure it. If they happened to close the breech, it had a tendency to go off when least expected, without pulling the trigger. They would only close the breech when they were getting ready to use it.

We had been pounding the ground for quite awhile and feeling shitty, hot, and ornery, when Weyant started on me with his New York crooked smile.

"Red, has anyone ever told you that you have really a nice ass for a guy? That's all I can look at; I can't get my eyes off that nice ass of yours. It bubbles so nice from side to side. I fall asleep at night and that's all I ever see, over and over again." You get the drift. Pretty soon everyone is hacking on everyone else and Weyant hasn't quit either. After I'd had enough, I made him walk in front of me. I told him if he opened his mouth just once more, I'd riddle his ass with so many holes, he wouldn't know which one to stick his head up and which one to look out of.

Weyant and I were going at each other pretty good when just then I heard a *thook*. I felt something hit me in the back and bounce off into the rice paddy on my right side. I turned around and looked at Hester and he looked almost white! He eyes were as big as silver dollars, his jaw nearly dropped down to his chest, holding his breath. "You shot me...Damn you, Hester, you...shot me!" Sure as hell, he had closed the breech on his M79 and it went off.

No damage was done. For a rocket-propelled grenade to explode, it has to spin through the air thirty meters to arm itself before it will explode on impact. He had hit me in my barrel bag and then it ricocheted off one of my C-ration cans. It landed in the rice paddy, buried in the water and mud. That put the kibosh on all the trash talk.

Well, it wasn't long after that before Hester started telling the story of how he shot me in the back and it hit my barrel bag, right where I had put my rosary. It was a miracle! The more we walked, the more the story grew. It must have made the rounds with all of Hester's buddies later on, because every time I ran into one of them, they would just laugh and shake their heads. I think everyone was getting a good laugh about it.

More than forty years later, he's probably still telling that story. Hester was part of our squad for awhile and we went through a lot together. Hester and I once got caught on the wrong end of friendly fire from a helicopter. We were in some heavy action when our platoon leader wanted my M60 and Hester's M79 to provide firepower along a tree line to help secure troops sweeping through from the right. Just as we were moving in, a chopper had opened up on this tree line, and Hester and I couldn't move fast enough to get out of the way. We both fell forward into the water just as bullets were hitting and dancing a few feet ahead of us...that was a close one! I remember Hester was about ready to take out that chopper if he came around again. We found out later that our platoon leader had ordered us in so we would be further from a certain enemy KIA. Our platoon leader wanted to get to this enemy KIA, who had a pistol on him that he wanted to take for a souvenir, before we did. Turns out Anderson got it instead.

I don't know what happened to Hester. I got sick and ended up in the hospital, and when I returned, he was gone. I assumed he was off line, waiting to go home. I think about him also.

My rosary survived the war, although it was in pretty rough shape by the end. Marcia put together a shadow box of some medals and other memorabilia, including my rosary, which she had fixed. To this day, it still gives me a great deal of comfort to look at my rosary and see that it's still doing what it did best—it's around my dog tags!

21

Evacuated Again

I HAD BEEN ON LINE just short of seven months when I got really sick. By this time, I was an old timer. I had gone through several platoon leaders, platoon sergeants, and ammo bearers, and everyone in the platoon except me was new.

At that time, one of my platoon leaders wanted to put together a Special Forces Operations Platoon. There were no snipers in our battalion but there was an in-country thirty-day sniper school program. Our old 2-6 talked to Addington, Beck, and me since we'd been there the longest and he knew us well. He wanted us to attend the sniper school so we could be part of his Special Forces Platoon. Both Addington and Beck decided to go, but I didn't think I would be a good candidate because when I used my M60 I never aimed at anything anyway. I always felt that my main job was just to throw out a lot of lead.

With Addington and Beck gone to sniper school, I hardly knew anyone in my platoon anymore and it seemed my odds of survival were not good. I was the last of the last, becoming more and more of a loner. Our squad was about half the size of what it used to be, basically a skeleton squad. We had a thirty-day shake n' bake squad leader who was so new, he still sparkled. He was a good guy but he knew nothing and referred any decisions to me and a few other guys. All of this led to the second time in the war when I was totally petrified.

We were moving by truck from one location to another. I felt vulnerable, like any minute, during this huge troop movement, somebody on a scooter would ride by and toss a grenade into the middle of our truck. Because I'd been around the longest of anyone on the truck, I didn't have the confidence in them that I should have. I didn't think they were being alert enough or that they knew what to watch for. I froze up. Several guys even asked me if I was okay. I knew then I needed to snap out of it, to tell myself I wasn't dead and to quit worrying about it—it worked, though it took every mental, physical, emotional, and spiritual bone in mind and body to keep going. I was never so glad to reach our destination and get off those trucks. I felt the safest when we were pounding the ground.

The monsoon season was slowly abating a bit by this time but my feet were still in pretty bad shape. Insect repellant turns your skin hard (it's 100% Deet, which eats plastic, clothes, and canvas) and I was dealing with that too...whether I should use it, or not use it and risk malaria.

One night as we were setting up our nightly ambush site, I could see we were in for more rain. Many of us carried a small hammock. All the VC and NVA soldiers had one, made of parachute material from our artillery flares, so we'd take them off enemy KIA. Once in awhile when we were in an ambush site, you'd be able to find a spot to string a hammock where it would be hidden, close to the ground, and you could string your poncho over it like a tent. I'd always keep my M60 right next to me. That night I was able to pull my poncho over my hammock and hoped like hell we wouldn't blow a bush. Soon the rain started, and it poured nonstop. I wasn't exactly staying dry, but I wasn't lying in the mud either.

I got up the next morning and I knew something was terribly wrong. I could hardly stand and kept falling down on my right side. My head hurt, and I was very nauseous, dizzy, shaking uncontrollably, and sweating. We hadn't blown a bush that night, but our other squad did. I was so out of it I didn't even notice.

We started to move out, but I couldn't walk without falling over. I even fell off the dike we were marching on. We were close to a road and only a couple clicks from the 2/47th firebase, so our platoon RTO man dispatched a Red Cross vehicle from there to come and get me and take me to a hospital, which was quicker than dispatching a dustoff chopper. They dropped me off at the fire base and then shipped me off to a hospital in Saigon.

I don't remember much of the trip there, other than a lot of waiting and watching. The hospital was a meat-grinder—a huge room with lots of activity. I saw what doctors and nurses went through in triage every day. You heard two phrases, repeated over and over: "Am I going to die?" and "Don't let me die!" All wounded went through there—enemy POWs right next to wounded and dead American soldiers. Some bodies looked like they were probably dead when they arrived. Some had died halfway through surgery and were just left there. Vietnamese doctors worked on all Vietnamese, be it north or south, and they were butchers. American doctors worked on all the rest, along with a few American, but mostly Filipino and Thai nurses.

I could see a couple of POWs being worked on by Vietnamese doctors. From what I saw, I wanted nothing to do with them. Each POW had a Vietnamese MP guard with them, and even they were some cruel bastards. It was a bloody mess. If someone died on the operating table and was removed, a little Vietnamese guy came by with a bucket of water, threw it on the table, and quickly wiped it down so it was ready for the next slab of meat. They reminded me of a butcher block table. They were only about five feet long and maybe only two feet wide, made out of wood two-by-fours nailed together.

The next thing I knew, I was on a table with no one around me, just lying there ready to pass out. "The room was a-spinnin'." Next to me was an old lifer who had just had or was having a heart attack. The doctors and nurses were working on him, using the defibrillator. I can still hear them say, "Stand clear of patient," and then zap-bang-pow, they'd light this poor guy right up. His arms and legs would stiffen out straight as a board and stay that way until they zapped him again, over and over. He made it through. The doctors and nurses were talking to him afterwards and telling him how they had lost him a couple of times but he was doing just fine and he was going home. His tour of duty was over.

My condition seemed like nothing next to all of this, but it wasn't long before the doctors and nurses were working on me. I was worried, not knowing what to expect. I thought I had come down with malaria. But that was quickly ruled out, which worried me even more. The doctors and nurses were reassuring and before long they let me know I had hepatitis, which is usually contracted from drinking contaminated water. In the field, we treated our drinking water with iodine tablets, then mixed in a little Kool-Aid with it, and we never had a problem. But I had most likely caught it from what we called "Vietnamese soup." Whenever we had the chance, we would trade some of our C's for this soup, which was basically ramen noodles with rice and fresh vegetables, a nice spice, and some greens. I liked it a lot, but apparently I'd had it one too many times.

I was put in the part of the hospital with all the malaria patients. The hospital itself was nothing more than a string of about a dozen Quonset buildings connected by a hallway. I don't remember too much of anything for the next several days other than the fact there were some other pretty sick guys around me. I do clearly remember wearing the blue cotton flannel pajamas and taking hot showers and how nice that was.

I also remember the gal that ran that part of the hospital. Her name was Major Garbolic, no lie. She was a short, heavy-set gal, obviously a lifer. She wore army fatigues instead of a nurse's uniform. She had huge breasts that stuck straight out, forming a six-inch flat shelf. She ran a tight ship, barking out orders to anyone who got out of line, always with a Lucky Strike cigarette stuck in her mouth. Cigarette ashes would fall on this boob shelf of hers so it was covered in a solid mass of gray.

One morning, after I was feeling a little better, I was sitting in a chair in the sun outside my Quonset building, which opened up to a courtyard of sorts. The next thing I knew, General Westmoreland and a photographer were standing next to me. General Westmoreland was the commanding general of the entire Vietnam War.

At first I was startled, and I didn't know who it was. He looked at me like I was a swamp creature. I felt he just wanted to have his picture taken with me and move on. It was the first time I felt dismissed, expendable, a future casualty of war—meat! His photographer took our picture, handed it to me, and awkwardly departed.

Looking at the picture, I was disheveled with long scraggily hair and a big scraggily mustache. As the general was walking away, I heard my sidekick say, "That was fun," and I replied, "Yeah!" Then he said, "Asshole," I said, "Yeah," again.

This hospital complex was interesting. In the evenings all the patients, if they felt up to it, could assemble in a small courtyard to watch movies. There was another Quonset hospital wing to the right of the one I was in. There was a fence about twenty feet high with concertino wire and then more Quonset buildings. I thought it was a little strange to have it fenced off, until I learned that was where all the POW patients were housed.

The first night I felt like watching a movie everyone moved a chair into the courtyard, including POW patients. We all wore blue pajamas, and you'd never have known before we came there we were trying to kill each other. During the day there was a lot of interaction between the two groups.

One day I ask if there was any particular reason why we were housed with POW patients other than they also needed medical care. I was surprised to learn it was so the hospital would not get hit with any incoming mortars or rockets. That also explained why none of the hospital Quonset buildings were fortified.

I was slowly getting my strength back, and I knew by then Major Garbolic was dismissing patients as soon as possible. She always knew just when we were healthy enough to go back to the field to kill or be killed.

22

SPECIAL FORCES OPERATIONS

WHEN I RETURNED TO MY platoon, they were in the process of trading locations with another battalion. My squad was also being changed up, and I gave up my M60. I had an opportunity to do something different. It was good timing as far as I was concerned.

Addington and Beck had returned from sniper school while I was in the hospital, and I had been on several operations in our new AO. When they returned, they were assigned to the Special Forces Operations Platoon led by one of our former platoon leaders, as I mentioned before. Our operations would be intensified in the Plain of Reeds again, and I was asked if I would be interested in putting together a small squad to assist snipers on small special operations in this area.

There was one more sniper besides Addington and Beck, and they rotated with each mission. Two would be on assignment while one would stand down on ready reserve. I had a small squad consisting of only five people and one radio. We would be assisting the snipers and their mission in a support capacity, to engage the enemy only when necessary. We would

Special Forces Support Squad – Manny, Miller, Myself,
Keefer, and Myers

be briefed on all operations—which would be a nice change. I was able to fill the positions by talking to some guys I knew. It was like having part of our old squad back together again.

My squad would also be on rotation with several others to assist in other special operations. As it turned out, it was easy duty. We continued to report and be assigned to our original platoon as always, but were called upon whenever Special Operations needed our assistance.

On each and every operation, the snipers and I were briefed on what the mission was and what we could expect. I always knew where we would be located before hand and most importantly, I felt confident HQ would have it marked on their big map and not make any mistakes. I knew who was around me and how far away they were. I knew where our mortar and artillery support was coming from and what the coordinates were. Since our mission was always to support the snipers' mission and only engage the enemy as a last resort, we also had an escape route, which was nice!

Throughout this major offensive, our squad worked in one area with the snipers, and it was high and dry. We always set up in one of about a half a dozen locations along a road that was frequently used by both us and the enemy. As the saying went, "We own the day, they own the night"—though we only ran these missions at night.

We would watch for enemy movement on this road and on a major canal that ran parallel to it. If we saw enemy movement, we would call it in as intel and the snipers would determine whether or not to engage. It all depended upon their mission. Many times, we just watched and reported. The snipers would only engage if it was determined the enemy was setting booby traps, if the enemy element was very small, or if a single Sampan was trying to maneuver toward our position. The snipers would make their shot and we would not move or in any way give away our position.

Throughout the course of this offensive, there were many small skirmishes and several major battles. After one particular firefight, the upper brass wanted the entire enemy KIA found, picked up, and brought in for inspection. This was done periodically. I was lucky enough not to ever have to do this. As it turned out, there were several days in a row where there was a high enemy body count each day. They were all to be brought in for inspection. After that, the army tried—so we were told—to ethically disposes of the dead bodies by throwing them in a pile, adding helicopter fuel, and cremating them.

My squad was assigned as backup to the snipers who watched the cremation site at night for enemies who might try to remove some of the bodies or to booby trap them or the area around the site.

One of the guys in my squad, Manny, always did his job and kept a low profile, but he did what he damn pleased. He could get away with it too. This was the wild, wild west. As the saying went, "What are they going to do to you, send you to Vietnam?" Your only guide was your internal guide. Manny was one of those guys that every time you told him to do something, he just smiled at you—with this permanent, devious smile that drove me crazy. On this occasion, I felt he crossed the line.

I had heard he wanted an enemy skull for some sort of for a skull-and-crossbones display. Most of the squad knew about it. I heard he wanted to "harvest" one from one of the dead bodies that we were watching on our nightly missions. I've heard of worse, but I wouldn't allow it while I was squad leader and he was in my squad.

His plan was to take one, place it in a plastic bag, put it in his backpack, and bury it next to our platoon bunker, where he could dig it up later. I told him that wasn't going to happen while I was his squad leader. He just looked at me and smiled. I repeated myself, using some pretty strong words. Of course it didn't mean a damn thing to him, but I was foolish enough to believe it did. Later that night, as we were in position, I heard this chopping sound, and immediately went on alert. Then someone said, "Its Manny!"

To this day, I can't get that sound out of my head. It'll flash to the surface in an instant. I sometimes feel as if I failed. I even think that if Okay Okay was my guardian, somehow we both failed.

23

FIRE BASE GETTYSBURG

WE CONTINUED IN OUR role as sniper support until our battalion rotated with another and we moved to a different AO. It would be a bit before we were called up again. With our new AO, we no longer rode the Tango boats out of Ben Luc on nighttime missions once a week, but the Special Forces did, including the snipers.

I believe I mentioned along with Beck and Addington there was a third sniper, named Shanley. We got to know him a bit; he was from California and guys called him "Shamming Shanley."

Beck and Shanley were on patrol with the Tango boats when they were hit with enemy small arms and rocket fire. Both were wounded, with Shanley getting the worst of it. We heard that Beck was hit in his hand, arm, shoulder, and upper back. They were both lucky, though. Neither one wore a helmet, and they didn't drown. Their injuries allowed them to be evacuated to Japan for surgery and then on to the States. So we lost Beck, and we would soon lose Addington too.

My time was getting shorter and shorter. One rule that dated back to the WWII era was that brothers could not serve together in the same war. When I first shipped over to Vietnam, I told a younger brother to volunteer as soon as possible for the army so he would be stationed somewhere else. That way if I came home, for whatever reason, he would not be sent to Vietnam.

He was dragging his feet about it, even though he was doing nothing else at the time. He eventually signed up, but was a little too late. About the time my overseas tour was nearing completion, my brother was finishing up training and ready to be issued orders for his overseas tour of duty.

The military was keenly aware of this, and would wait to assign one brother until the other returned, in some cases over two months. They were called "hold-overs," and would spend their days painting parking lots. This is exactly what they were doing with my brother, but I had a counter move to play.

The army was offering what they called the "180-day early out program," which said if your twelve-month tour duty was up in Vietnam, you could extend your overseas obligation for as many days as it took to be within 180 days of your two-year active service obligation. If I were to extend just under two more months in Vietnam, I would also be through with active service and not have to serve an additional five months state-side going crazy. In other words, I would serve one year, seven months, and three days of active duty.

If I did this, the army would have to cut orders for my younger brother for a location other than Vietnam. In the end this is what I did, but it would take my folks contacting their state representative for the army to send my brother to Germany. Who knows how long they were planning on holding him there.

I was looking forward to getting out five months early, and it looked like it would be smooth sailing until my orders for home came through. It took us awhile to settle in at our new base and AO, but we were enjoying ourselves and hitting the suds. We were doing small reconnaissance patrols, a few nighttime ambush operations, but mostly we were still just taking snipers out on nighttime missions. These trips were nothing more than glorified outer security—camping out under the stars outside the perimeter fence. The next day we'd come in, get drunk, then go back out and do it all over again!

Just when I thought I could start my short-timers' calendar, everything changed. We began hearing about something called the Cambodian Campaign. American troops would be initiating air and ground attacks on the Ho Chi Ming Trail just inside the Cambodian border. The first thing that went through my mind was this wasn't going to be good. I was so close...so close! It took the spirit out of me to think of the danger we'd be heading into.

It proved to be not as bad as I anticipated. I assembled my recon squad, and we joined all the other support squads plus the Special Forces Platoon. We were to be the forward element securing a fire base called "Fire Base Gettysburg." Gettysburg was first occupied by the 1st Calvary Division, and I was told it was somewhere close to the border. The definition of "close" turned out to be questionable.

Our squads were flown into Gettysburg at midday by what

*Gettysburg – Special Ops with Nui Ba Den (Black Virgin)
Mountain in the background*

had to be fifty helicopters. We learned it had already been swept for mines and booby traps, which made our jobs much easier. We established a perimeter, ground communications, and an ammo depot. There were several guard towers where we would set up with the snipers. It was in this desolate area that we saw for the first time what it looks like after an area is sprayed with Agent Orange, then hit with napalm.

I've seen a lot of areas sprayed by only Agent Orange and a lot hit only by napalm, but this was totally different. We were always told Agent Orange was 100 percent 2-4D, the same stuff used in small doses to kill dandelions. Gettysburg was a big dirt spot surrounded by absolutely bare ground for one click in all directions. That's a little over 1.25 miles across. The area was first sprayed with Agent Orange, to kill everything—and I mean everything. Then they waited about a month for the vegetation to dry and dropped napalm, burning everything down to little bits and pieces of charcoal.

At Gettysburg we lived in "rat holes," tunnels dug into the ground and covered with metal sheets and sand bags. We patrolled the whole area. Once we thought everything was secure, the rest of the battalion would fly in. As waves of helicopters were landing, troops were assembling, double-checking their gear and moving out into the unknown. The small support squads and snipers were to stay at Gettysburg, securing both the perimeter and the surrounding area with small recon patrols. It was rough conditions, though at least it was dry. Most of our feet were in bad shape from the wet jungle, and we were able to wear sandals to let our feet heal, which was nice for a change.

Our involvement in any heavy action was limited because of the area we were in. As I mentioned before, the southern battle zones were different than the northern zones. Our company would make contact with an NVA unit twice and we didn't even know if we were in Cambodia or not. Several other companies were hit hard in a heavy firefight with both VC and NVA forces.

Our involvement would expand closer and closer to the Cambodian border and the Black Virgin Mountain, or so we thought. Black Virgin was suspected of having an entrenched battalion of either Viet Cong or NVA. We were again asked to provide support for the snipers' mission, but we all knew that what we were really supposed to do was watch and recon only. The snipers did not want to engage, and it wouldn't have made any sense to do so.

The date of my departure from Vietnam was getting closer, and I was starting to think I might make it out in one piece. Then one day when I least expected it, my orders showed up. Usually, you're told by a superior officer your orders are in and when to report to Brigade HQ. From then on, I stayed with the snipers up in the towers during the day and in a rat hole at night. There were two guys from other platoons who also received their orders to return home.

Addington disappeared suddenly and I never asked where he was, assuming he was standing down or on another mission. I wouldn't find out until later that he shipped out on an emergency leave. Apparently his wife was either having a baby or she had a baby and there were complications. When my squad heard of this, we said he wasn't coming back. I hadn't known he was even married.

I hoped that everything was going well for Addington, but the thought that stuck in my mind was that if Addington had been KIA he would still have left a mark on the world because he had been married and they'd had a baby. I found myself envious of him and anyone else who was in the same position. I remember writing my sister and telling her about what I was thinking. I told her if I was killed, I would not have made a mark on this world and no one would remember me. I told her that I was hoping to make it home, but if I was killed she should make sure everyone would remember me because I wanted the ladies to serve giant hot ham and cheese sandwiches with at least a half-inch piece of ham on each and every sandwich at my funeral. I liked ham sandwiches. I felt I didn't have any identity. If anyone back home ever talked about me, they would always refer to me as one of "Schtop and Ardella's boys"—those were my parents' names.

After thinking about all of this for awhile, I started looking forward to the future. I wanted to go back to school, get married, and most of all have a couple of kids to make a mark and have a family. Okay-Okay felt okay with that.

Addington eventually came back from leave, but he wasn't the same guy at all. Something was obviously wrong. He refused to talk to almost anyone, and he and I never talked again.

The last we saw of each other he was about half-way up the ladder on a sniper tower. I spotted him, but he just glanced at me and kept climbing. Nobody wants to say hello; then you don't have to say good-bye.

One other note on Gettysburg—when I attended my first 5/60th reunion forty-three years later, the speaker displayed a huge map of our AO, identifying all the various base locations, areas of operation, stand-down areas, and fire bases. Fire Base Gettysburg was not shown on this map. Someone asked the speaker about it, and the speaker asked for a show of hands of anyone who was at Gettysburg. There were about twenty of us. The speaker then informed us that no one knows where Fire Base Gettysburg is located! To this day it remains a mystery. Many of us talked later and we all agreed we never knew where we were and what direction we were in relation to certain landmarks. When our battalion moved from one location at Roc Kein to another at Binh Phouc, we thought we were moving north when we really were moving southwest into more jungle. We were told Fire Base Gettysburg was close to Black Virgin Mountain, which was close to if not right on the border of Cambodia. We now suspect that since we could see Black Virgin, we were on the Cambodian side of the border. At the time we didn't know the difference and didn't ask.

24

GOING HOME

IT SEEMED SURREAL TO think that I was actually going home. I had been in Vietnam so long, been through so much, seen so much, lived through so much, that I felt detached from my life in this place called America, that was supposed to be my real home.

Three of us hopped on a departing helicopter heading for the 25th Division Brigade HQ and from there hopped another to our Battalion HQ, where we tried to get our thoughts and feelings in order before heading home. I was anxious, yet I wanted to stay as mellow as possible, so I kept myself in a state of inebriation with other short timers.

There was not much else to do to get ready. I got a haircut, the first of three in four days. I took two sets of fatigues to Mama San's laundry, turned in my M16, my 45 pistol, and last but not least, my trusty helmet. It had been my pillow, shovel, chair, water bucket, umbrella, stool, hammer, hiding place, sink, map, and companion. In its place I donned an army base-ball cap. Some of us went to the village to Susie's Coke Stand and Wild West Saloon, aka "the yellow house," to trade in the last of our menthol cigarettes we'd been saving for black market barbecued USDA choice T-bone steak, medium rare.

My day had arrived. I took my last cold shower to sober up, picked up my laundry, said good-bye to the other short timers, and headed for the front gate. Along the way, I stopped at the chapel. I sat down just inside the tent cover, and there, for the first time ever, I felt uncomfortable and couldn't close both eyes. I wept and wept, and Okay Okay was truly with me. I realized at that moment I would never be the same person I was before. I had lost too much. What was this other world that I was going back too?

I made it to the front gate and waited for the first jeep or truck heading for Brigade HQ. One of the gate guards turned out to be a buddy of mine from my old squad who had been wounded and landed this job. He knew what the jeep schedule was and said he would get me the best ride. Before long, I was on my way. In less than two days, I would be "home," out of Vietnam, out of the army, in a place called Iowa, on a small farm.

Once I arrived at Brigade HQ, the army bullshit started. Maybe it was a good thing...mind control, you know. First thing was that everyone had to get a haircut, period. I must have gone into a catatonic state, because I don't remember much of my time there. I do remember looking at the airplane that was to take us to the Tan Son Nhut airbase and wondering if it would get us there. I say "us," but don't remember anyone who was with me specifically.

I arrived at Tan Son Nhut and sat in an open area used for the airport terminal, just off a runway, when a big "freedom bird" pulled up. That was my ride "home," and I could hardly wait to board that plane. My sidekick-companion-guardian said, "Hee yeah!" I boarded the plane and felt shocked seeing American flight attendants all dressed up, smelling of perfume. They must have sensed my disorientation, because they were overly gracious, trying to comfort us. They repeated to all of us, "You're going home, you're going home." They showed more emotion than we did, but I think we were just trying to convince ourselves that this was really happening.

It was a long ride back to our discharge location, the airbase in Oakland, California. We had a smooth flight with a slight tail wind and a stopover in Alaska. It was a quiet flight—we spoke to the flight attendants, not much to each other. We landed in Oakland in the early morning, so we couldn't see much of this "new world" we had heard about. We all assembled in the mess hall for breakfast before we began processing out.

After a nice breakfast (real eggs), we got rid of the old, rotten fatigues we were wearing. I was never happier than when I said good-bye to those God-forsaken jungle boots. Never again would I ever wear jungle boots, never! We were given a pair of shorts and packed off to the "hot" showers. Man, it was nice to take a shower with clean water and hot water. I know I had dirt in places that hadn't seen water for a year.

My shaving cream turned brown and my face, for the first time in fourteen months, didn't feel sweaty and greasy. From there, it was off to the barber again, where they couldn't find anything to cut. We were then measured for our army dress greens. Next, we got our medical exam. I was in good health except that I lost a lot of my hearing. I had damage in both ears, with my right ear the worst. We were told what to do to have our teeth fixed at our local dentist when we got home.

Then I did something I would later regret, though apparently every other Vietnam returnee did the same. I didn't read all of my discharge papers. I glanced at some, and saw some inaccuracies. So what if they had my blood type wrong, or if I had a Vietnam campaign medal or not? They even had my name spelled wrong, but I didn't care. Every one of us just started signing papers as fast as we could and didn't ask any questions.

Next we were given all our discharge papers and our ticket for home. We were getting close. We went to pick up our army dress greens. We lined up to be dressed and fitted, and at the end of the line we were decked out in our new army dress greens with all the bells and whistles, medals, brass buttons, and ribbons galore.

The strangest part of it all was wearing underwear, a belt, a tie, and socks with dress shoes! After not wearing underwear and socks for a year, it felt pretty uncomfortable, but I kept telling myself I wouldn't be getting ring worm anymore!

The last and final step was that we were all entitled to a big thick steak. By the time we sat down to have our steak meal, it was late afternoon. Everyone was antsy and not conversing. I ordered my steak, and it came shortly thereafter with all the fixings, but it was still half frozen. Just then, someone stood up and asked if we should just grab a cab for the airport. I stood up with some other guys and said, "Let's just go."

We arrived at the airport, worried we might be confronted by protesters. It was even suggested we change out of our dress greens to avoid any sort of harassment. However, it proved to be uneventful. I spent most of the night at the airport waiting to catch an early morning flight out. There were probably a dozen of us hanging out together, waiting to catch flights to all corners of the country. No one knew anyone else, but we all felt the same. We just wanted to go home.

I boarded my flight for Minneapolis, and it was clear sailing the whole way. The plane landed early on July 14, 1970. I had to make arrangements to catch a shuttle flight to Rochester, and from there I was planning to call home and wait to be picked up. I didn't want to take any chances calling ahead of time, just in case something happened to delay me.

I never encountered any protesters or bad language. As a matter of fact, it was just the opposite. I hit the first bar I could find that was open and the bartender said I could have anything I wanted to drink—it was on the house. We chatted for awhile and I told him it was a culture shock stepping out into the civilian world. Everybody had long hair and was wearing long dresses and granny glasses to look cool. He said that's only the half of it!

From the bar, I called my sister who I believe was still going to school in the Twin Cities. She immediately came to the airport to see me and we had the best visit ever. We talked and talked, and it was quite emotional. We both lost track of time, when all of a sudden we realized my flight was already boarded and ready for departure to Rochester. My sister told me to head for the terminal and that she would try to hold the plane for me, which she did. Apparently she gave them "a soldier is returning home" story.

This was the last leg of my flight home, and it was surreal... I didn't feel ready to see anyone just yet and thought maybe I should have stayed in Oakland for a week to somehow prepare myself for all the change. I felt alone in a strange world.

It's a short flight to the Rochester airport from Minneapolis, and we were barely in the air when we were already preparing to land. Once at Rochester, the first thing I did was hit the bar again, and the bartender asked if this was my last stop. I said it was, and I didn't know if I was quite ready for it.

I must have looked like some character because drinks were on the house again. From there I called home and I can't remember who took the call or what I said or any of the conversation. I must have told them I was in Rochester, but I couldn't remember who was coming to get me, when they were coming, or even if anybody was coming. When I came back to the bar, the bartender asked me how it went. He must have thought I was totally in the bag because I said I didn't know and that I might be there for awhile.

After about an hour or so, I got up to fetch my duffel bag when I saw my mother, the old man, and my little sister come through the terminal doors. It was a stiff moment for me. I told them that I thought I would never, ever see them again.

My older sister always knew what was going on with me, but I never told my folks what to expect or what to prepare for. Everything was a blur at this point until I returned to my old, new, different home. I do remember getting a nod from the bartender as I gazed out to the west over the runway and then turned to gather my gear and left.

It was a long, quiet ride home. I withdrew a little, I remember, trying to absorb the countryside and process where I was now and what it was like and what it looked like thirty-six hours ago. I was doing fine until we turned in the driveway.

I can remember my little sister, just twelve years old at the time, when we first looked at each other at the airport. But it was as we were turning in the driveway that she patted my knee and said, "You're going to be okay, okay...you're going to be okay."

25

STARTING OVER

NEXT CAME THE HARD PART. Being around death and dying almost seemed easy, because I didn't have to think about anything else. It was just a matter of time and nothing I did or didn't do could change it. How was I going to start living all over again?

I can't recall much of anything the first couple of days I was home. I'm sure I indulged in as many ham sandwiches as I could stand—dream fulfilled. I got my younger brother's car washed and running again so I had a set of wheels. Quite a few high school buddies stopped over to see me, and several of them were also Vietnam veterans so we had a lot to talk about. They told me about an upcoming lake party where there would be lots of people.

I loved civvies, especially blue jeans, T-shirts, socks, and a new pair of tennis shoes. I was even getting used to jockey shorts. Before I had the chance to unwrap my two sets of fatigues I had laundered in Vietnam, my mother said she wanted to wash them again. When she was done she said she'd seen dirty clothes before and really black water in the washing machine, but she had never seen before such dirty and foul-smelling water as that which resulted from washing my army fatigues. I think she washed them again, and they came out nice and soft. Probably my buddies in Vietnam were right. At Mama San's laundry, she washed everyone's clothes in the green lagoon and pressed them with buffalo urine.

I did a lot of restless sleeping the first couple of days, and I called my girlfriend so we could get together over the weekend. I was a little apprehensive about seeing her for the first time in fourteen months. We certainly had our difficulties during our time apart. I would get letters from her, but it was impossible for me to write back until I was back at base where it was dry, which meant it was often a long time between my letters. It didn't help either that I chose to take my R&R in Australia rather than Hawaii, where she wanted to meet me. Her dad also passed away suddenly from a massive heart attack while I was overseas, which caused a lot of difficulty for us. She was having a rough time of it and I felt sorry for her.

The few days I had before we were to meet, I spent recuperating and thinking about how it would be seeing her again after such a long time. What would I say, what should I say, and what would I do? Should I try to be warm when I didn't know how to be warm anymore?

I wasn't ready for any big, climactic moments when our eyes would meet and we would fall into each other's arms with hugs and kisses—no way José. I didn't have emotion left in me, and I felt like I had to start over again with living and life.

We finally met that Saturday and it was awkward, but it felt good to hug and begin to feel something again. We spent the weekend together and it was great. I felt being together got me started healing. After that, we spent every weekend and sometimes more together. I would drive down to Des Moines to see her during the week and drive back home Sunday night or Monday morning.

I thought everything was going fine with us when I left for home one Sunday afternoon, but we would never see each other again. When the mail arrived that Monday I received my first and only "Dear John" letter. I have to be the only sap I know of who got a "Dear John" letter from his girlfriend three weeks *after* he got home from Vietnam. What a kick in the head. Then again, I could understand. Fourteen months was too long and too much to make up for. Apparently she had met someone else and was getting married. I didn't even have a clue—I didn't pick up a single sign, and they should have been everywhere! Later on in the day when I thought she would be home from work, I called her apartment and talked to her roommate. I was told she had quit her job some time ago and moved out overnight without telling her roommate where she was going. Our time together was all a ruse and she didn't miss one trick, or make one mistake. This just confirmed that I truly was starting over.

After this, my youngest brother would be the support I needed, and he helped me the most. He never asked any questions but was always there for me. We spent a lot of time together, getting to know each other and having a good time. He turned out to be quite a character, and is a true friend to this day.

Another huge change after my return was my relationship with my old man. I hadn't seen him hardly at all since sixth grade, and when we did meet, it was volatile. The day that I came home from Vietnam was the day I felt I was born in his eyes. He suddenly treated me like I was a human being and listened to what I had to say. He was a completely different person around me.

I asked my mother one day what was with him. Her response gave me the shock of my life. She said he was petrified of me! Petrified, I asked? She said yes, and she couldn't explain it either, but he didn't know what to expect from me or what I might do to him. I thought that was crazy, but I wasn't about to try to change his mind, because it was finally going well for us. We would continue to have a good father-and-son relationship until his death. I think starting over was beneficial for the both of us.

I felt fortunate coming home to the community and environment that I did. Friends and neighbors were lifesavers for me. I thought no one knew who I was, but I was wrong. Young men and their wives who were a little older than me were concerned about the safety of their neighbors who were Vietnam veterans. Several ladies in the neighborhood played a big part in helping me through bad times. Whenever we met they were always happy to see me and concerned about how I was doing. Their husbands told me if I ever needed anything, all I had to do was ask.

I also found out that these women were my mother's support team during low times when I was away. If she didn't hear from me for awhile, like when I was in the field for a long stretch, my mother would be a basket case. My little sister would walk to the mailbox every day, and my mother would watch from the kitchen window to see if she was running back up the driveway to the house. If she was running, it meant she had a letter from me. My sister told me many days she walked back to the house to find her crying over the kitchen sink. Apparently she cried a lot and lost a bunch of weight.

My uncle Gene always wanted to know the latest news about me as well. They told me he called often, and my mother called him every time she got a letter from me. He wanted to know everything I had to say, and even wanted to put it in the local newspaper. That was Uncle Gene! Knowing that my uncle and the neighbor ladies were there for my mother helped me when I came home.

In the following months, I spent a lot of time partying and drinking, and the rest of the time in a bar. It was an awkward time for me and for the people around me. The friends I had before going to Vietnam, also veterans, told me to stay away, that I made them nervous. No problem, good-bye.

A high school buddy of mine was going off to school and said I could ride his old Harley Davidson motorcycle all I wanted while he was gone. I found a few other guys to bum around with who had bikes, and sometimes I would just take off by myself and see the country. The party scene was fun, but it was taking its toll.

I was getting tired of the drinking, tired of the village queens, tired of bar flies, tired of strippers, tired of drunks, tired of fighting, tired of coming home bloodied, my new clothes in shreds, tired of not wanting to sleep, tired of just about everything. I really had to start over or I wasn't going to make it.

26

CONCLUSION

BECAUSE OF MY BROTHER and sister, I was able to hang on. I had lost track of Okay Okay, and I started to think it was time for me to find him. I had visions of him passed out in The Fall-In Angel Saloon. I knew it was going to take more than a song and a prayer for me to find him, because I'd worn him out and it was my turn to step up.

The turning point came about one day, when I was driving in the middle of nowhere, to somewhere I don't even remember, in my new Saab 99. As I was flipping between stations on my car radio, I happened to catch a talk by a governor of some state—I'm not even sure which one, possibly Ohio. He was a Vietnam veteran. He said, "Vietnam can do two things to you: it can make a better person of you or it can make a monster of you." That was all I heard, but I said to myself, "I don't want to be a monster," and my life changed in an instant. I felt I had found Okay Okay...I saw him lift his head and look at me. I didn't speak the word "Vietnam" for the next fifteen years.

A short time later I turned to another station. I don't know what made me stop there, because I was the unlikeliest audience for this particular speaker and topic, but I felt he was talking straight at me. It was the Reverend Jesse Jackson addressing a black audience on the subject "Down with Dope and Up with Hope." I don't remember much about the dope part, but the other half of the speech struck me. He spoke about the opportunities for making a good living, opportunities for an education, opportunities for a good job, opportunities for having a good family environment, opportunities for having your children go to a good school, opportunities for being in and enjoying good communities, opportunities for being in and involved with a church, opportunities to reach out. He said no one could stop what you can accomplish.

My first thought was racist. I didn't mean for it to be, but I thought that if his speech was about opportunity, even if he was speaking to a black audience, it sure as heck could apply to me as well. I knew what risk was, and the risks I took in Vietnam made the risks at home pretty safe. From then on, I just wanted to start living life. And I did—I did everything I could to see new things, learn new things, do new things, all on the outer edge of life where no one knew me. I could be out under the radar, taking risks, learning from my mistakes, and enjoying the rewards of my accomplishments. I helped out people I'd never met before, and it came back around a hundredfold. Even when I was just trying to keep my head down, people remembered me.

I would seek out old friends to make them new again. Maybe I couldn't change my life right away, but I could at least change my attitude.

I realized what war did to me, the change in me that I wasn't able to put my finger on—it's hate. Hate is painful, and the army and war has a way of making you hate. The training, the marching, all the stupid simulations of throwing hand grenades or hand-to-hand combat; it's all to make you hate and kill. We'd call our enemies gooks, slants, slits, dinks, ears, fish, skin, scalps, and any other body part we could think of. We needed to hunt-'em up, find-'em, shoot-'em, kill-'em, blow-'em up, search and destroy. We weren't even supposed to "destroy" inanimate objects, we "killed" them. After awhile, you start to hate yourself and everything around you. How do you kill hate, though? Hate slowly corrodes the container!

Attitude adjustment is not accomplished by drinking or getting smashed. I needed to go back to some vague plans I'd had earlier, during and right after the war. I'd never gotten serious about them, but now I wanted to make them real goals. The word "mark" always stuck in my head—I was envious of men with children and families. I knew I didn't have to do that right away, but I wanted to look for other ways to make my own mark.

I went back to school under the GI bill. This time I tried to improve on my study habits. I made new friends and met new people, including a large group of veterans also going to school on the GI bill that I would get to know. I met more people from other colleges too, and eventually that would lead me to a very special gal.

A college roommate of mine was dating a gal who was a knock-out. She introduced me to her best friend, Marcia, who was a bigger knock-out in my book. We had a lot of fun together, and she was the first of only a few who would ever punch a hole in the emotional armor I was accused of having. We still have fun to this day. She is more than I ever could have expected, more than I deserve, and I owe her so much. Marcia and I were married almost four years before we started our family.

We would have two delightful daughters with the most beautiful auburn hair you've ever seen. They grew up to be the nicest, most pleasant, absolutely beautiful young women you could ever meet. I always thought they had striking beauty, but that's maybe just because I'm Dad. I was the kind of dad that they would refer to as "the big easy," and that was just fine with me. They had me wrapped around their little fingers. They still do! Friends and family thought they looked just like Julie Ann Moore, Fergie, or Nicole Kidman.

My girls are everything to me. Even so, they've told me many times that there's something different about Dad. It was easy for me to strike the fear of God into boyfriends, but when it came to emotional support I fell short. Hearing that from them hurt, but apparently that's common for combat veterans. I had to work at it and still do.

Now they have families of their own, and it weighs on me heavily to think of my grandchildren going through what I went through. I want them to know that they already paid a price through me and to know it's not worth it to fight in a totally unwarranted war. It isn't glamorous. It accomplishes nothing! You lose the human part of "human being," and a sense of who you are or who you could have become. You don't look at yourself or others the same, and you lose all sense of fear. You just don't ever want to speak out, or peek out from behind that protective wall. It's a realization that you became "just meat."

Politicians don't understand and don't want to understand as long as it doesn't involve them or their family members. It isn't their loss. We combat veterans came home fully aware of our losses. WWII veterans already knew it, but it remained unspoken. We wouldn't talk about it, even to our children. Sometimes, it's just best to leave it alone. As far as my girls knew, their dad was a combination of Rambo with red hair and Mr. Dirt, and I fought under the 9th Infantry Division patch that looks like a psychedelic cookie.

This book is my attempt to honor WWII veterans by doing something they didn't—talk to their kids, grandkids, grand-nieces and nephews, and anyone else about how they would lose a part of who they are because of war.

If I'm still around and anyone wants to talk to me, about anything from politics, to guns, to gun control, to booby traps, to war, to what's really important—even some juicy secrets of war—we'll do it, okay? Okay!

LIST OF MILITARY TERMS:

ACV – air-cushion vehicle

AIT – advanced infantry
(or individual) training

AO – area of operations

ARVN – Army Republic of Vietnam
(South Vietnam Army)

AWOL – absent without leave

CO – commanding office

C's – c-rations

C-4 – plastic explosives

GI – government issued

G2 – military intelligence

HQ – headquarters

KIA – killed in action

LZ – helicopter landing zone

MIA – missing in action

MP – military police

NCO – non-commissioned officer

NVA – North Vietnamese Army

POW – prisoner of war

PZ – helicopter pickup zone

RPG – rocket propelled grenade

SP – one-hundred-man supply pack

USO – united services organization

VA – Veterans Administration

VC – Viet Cong (South Vietnam

militia gorilla forces)

WIA – wounded in action

2-1 – second platoon, first squad

2-2 – second platoon, second squad

2-4 – second platoon, platoon sergeant

2-6 – second platoon, platoon leader

CPSIA information can be obtained at www.ICGtesting.com
Printed in the USA
BVOW07s1651040814

361278BV00001B/14/P